Killing Peace

Garry M. Leech has worked and traveled extensively in Latin America during the past 22 years. He currently resides in New York City where he edits INOTA's online journal *Colombia Report* (www.colombiareport.org). His writings have appeared in numerous publications including *NACLA Report on the Americas*, *In These Times*, *Salon*, and *motherjones.com*.

Information Network of the Americas (INOTA) is a non-profit organization that seeks to promote social and economic justice throughout Latin America by fostering a greater awareness and understanding of U.S. foreign policy in the region. INOTA believes that easy and affordable access to information and analysis of U.S. foreign policy is essential if citizens are to effectively participate in the democratic process.

Killing Peace

Colombia's Conflict and the Failure of U.S. Intervention

Garry M. Leech

Information Network of the Americas (INOTA)

New York

Library of Congress Control Number: 2002105269

ISBN 0-9720384-0-X

Information Network of the Americas (INOTA)
P.O. Box 20314
New York, NY 10009
www.colombiareport.org

Printed and bound in the United States with 100% union labor

Typeset and designed by Sheep Meets Sheep Productions
Cover design by Debra Sahu Barron
Cover illustration by Peter C. Gentile

First printing April 2002

In memory of my father

Contents

Republic of Colombia

Acknowledgments

This book could not have been written without the generous help of many friends, relatives, and colleagues. I am indebted to Kevin Walter, whose tireless efforts, editing expertise, and vision were invaluable. I am extremely grateful to Thomas C. Wright, Mark Schapiro, Eric Fichtl, and Chris Cortier, for their close readings and keen suggestions, which added immeasurably to the final text. Sincere thanks go to Peter Gentile and Debra Sahu Barron for sharing their creative and technical skills. The Dick Goldensohn Fund generously supported much of my research in Colombia. Special thanks go to my many friends in Colombia who, for their own safety, must sadly remain anonymous. Most of all, I am forever indebted to my loving wife, Jacqueline Gentile, who has managed this project from start to finish and whose enduring support has made it all possible.

Acknowledgments

Introduction

The first casualty of our war on drugs has been historical perspective. The principal aim of this book is to situate the conflict in Colombia in the historical context from which it arose. To perceive Colombia simply as an exporter of cocaine or a perpetrator of terrorism is to completely misunderstand it, but the key failing of U.S. policy toward Colombia in the last decades has been to view it in precisely those terms. The U.S. has made Colombia the largest recipient of dollars and weapons in the Western Hemisphere under the guise of a war on drugs—and now terrorism—while refusing to address the political, social, and economic causes of the violence that has plagued Colombia for more than fifty years.

Over the years, I have been privileged to meet and learn from Colombians in many regions of their tragic, yet beautiful, country. I met Luis Hernández, who fled from his village in southern Bolívar to the relative safety of Barrancabermeja after paramilitary death squads killed his friends. On the border with Ecuador I talked with Cecilia Ramírez who, along with her family, abandoned their farm after their food crops were destroyed by aerial fumigation that was supposed to target illegal coca fields. In the small town of Zaragoza, in northeastern Antioquia, I listened to the story of Jorge Eliécer Rodríguez, who lost his left leg when he stepped on a landmine planted near his home. I have visited indigenous communities in Cauca whose economic plight has led them to cultivate opium poppies while being caught in the middle of the armed conflict. I have talked with army, guerrilla, and paramilitary commanders, whose words attempted to justify their hatred of the enemy, but whose actions have brought misery and death to thousands of innocent civilians.

The United States has the resources, influence, and—as an avowed champion of peace, human rights, and free markets—a stated interest in bringing about a peaceful settlement to the conflict in Colombia. Unfortunately, the United States has not been a partner for peace and development, and its involvement has only exacerbated an already dire situation. The picture of U.S. intervention in Latin America is painfully familiar. In the last fifty years, Washington has overthrown democratically elected governments in Guatemala and Chile; invaded the sovereign states of the Dominican Republic, Grenada and Panama; organized and funded the unsuccessful invasion of Cuba; supported brutal militaries allied with right-wing death squads in El Salvador, Guatemala and Argentina; and orchestrated a near decade-long illegal war against Nicaragua.

The United States has maintained close ties to the Colombian government since the early days of the Cold War, but it was not until the 1980s that the floodgates of U.S. money and weapons opened in the service of the "war on drugs." Since then, with only low-level coverage by the U.S. media and almost no public debate on the matter in this country, the United States has stepped deeper and deeper into Colombia's civil conflict—pouring in hundreds of millions of dollars of aid and arms, along with hundreds of military personnel—worsening the violence, threatening the fragile stability of the region, and increasing the suffering of the Colombian people. In 2000, as a solution to Colombia's worsening problems, the Clinton administration proposed yet another massive increase in military aid. The following year, the Bush administration continued this policy by proposing even more drug-war funding for Colombia's armed forces.

As if impoverished Colombians weren't suffering enough, the last decade has seen the implementation of a "new world order" economic plan imposed by Washington policymakers and international lending institutions with the acquiescence of the Colombian government. These neoliberal policies have contributed to Colombia's worst economic recession in more than half a century and an unemployment rate that is among the highest in Latin America.

The "war on terrorism" is the most recent and dangerous rationale for expanding U.S. involvement in Colombia's internal conflict. Foreign policy circles in Washington are abuzz with talk of Colombia's guerrillas as this hemisphere's greatest terrorist threat. The United States has always stopped short of the direct deployment of troops in Colombia, but the war on terrorism promises to be just the justification for such action that has so far been lacking.

This book addresses these issues in two roughly chronological parts. Part One, "Fifty Years of Violence," is a fully revised and expanded version of the essay by the same title that first appeared in the Internet journal *Colombia Report*. It deals with the history and the root causes of Colombia's violence, dating back to independence from Spain in 1819. The civil conflict, as we know it today, arose from the smoldering ashes of *La Violencia*, a spasm of politically motivated looting and killing that gripped the country from

1948 until 1958. This section also traces the beginnings of U.S. military ties with Colombia until the end of the 1990s when U.S. aid increased exponentially.

Part Two, "Colombia and the New World Order," begins with a brief history of the U.S. drug war and discusses the opening of the Colombian economy, which occurred as part of the post–Cold War globalization process during the 1990s. It analyzes the development of Plan Colombia, a multibillion-dollar international aid proposal to curtail drug trafficking, revive the nation's economy, and end the civil conflict. The Clinton administration's contribution to Plan Colombia was a $1.3 billion aid package that dramatically escalated the U.S. war on drugs. President Andrés Pastrana was elected to Colombia's highest office in 1998 on a platform of peace, which led to negotiations with the Revolutionary Armed Forces of Colombia (FARC). Finally, this section details the collapse of this peace process and traces Washington's justification for intervention in Colombia from the war on drugs to the new global war against terrorism.

PART ONE

Fifty Years of Violence

*Little by little, however, and as the war became
more intense and widespread, his image
was fading away into a universe of unreality.*

Gabriel García Márquez
One Hundred Years of Solitude

The Roots of the Violence

Unlike in any other Latin American country, Colombia's principal cities—Bogotá, Medellín, Cali, and Barranquilla—are separated from each other by vast expanses of towering mountain peaks and dense, lowland tropical jungles. Many of Colombia's provincial regions developed in relative isolation from the capital, Bogotá, and the outside world. Until the end of the 19th century it took less time to travel from the Caribbean port city of Cartagena across the Atlantic Ocean to Paris than to the nation's capital—seated on a savannah 8,600 feet up in the Andes Mountains. The rare occasions that rural Colombians had to deal with the national government usually involved confrontations with military forces operating in the interests of Bogotá's political and economic elite. This geographic isolation bred a distrust of central government that still persists in rural Colombia. To this day, the government in Bogotá has never effectively controlled all of the national territory.

Following independence from Spain in 1819, local landed elites, primarily white descendants of Spanish colonial rulers, held politi-

7

cal and economic sway throughout Colombia and retained control of the country's prime agricultural land. In essence, independence merely transferred rule over Colombia from Spanish colonial administrators to an oligarchy comprised of Spanish-descended Colombians serving their own political and economic interests.

By the mid-nineteenth century, Colombia's elite had formed two political parties—the Liberals and Conservatives—that would dominate Colombian politics until the end of the twentieth century. The Liberals favored a federalist system of government, separation of church and state, and laissez-faire economics, while the Conservatives preferred a strong central government, close ties between church and state, and a government actively involved in economic policy-making. But by the mid-twentieth century there was little difference between the two parties, especially regarding economic policy.

Despite the country's formidable geographic barriers, the two parties eventually managed to infiltrate many of Colombia's settled regions, although constituents usually displayed a greater allegiance to regional party officials than to the national government. Ideological differences between the Liberal and Conservative elite, both locally and nationally, frequently resulted in outbreaks of violence, pitting party loyalists from each faction against each other. While peasants routinely took part in Colombia's many civil wars, these conflicts were fundamentally between the interests of the ruling elite, not class-based liberation struggles. Peasants simply fought to protect the interests of their Liberal or Conservative *patron*—the local landowner.

The turbulence of the nineteenth century culminated with the 1899-1902 War of the Thousand Days. With Colombia's economy suffering from a decline in world coffee prices and Conservatives having held power since 1886, Liberals disputed the 1898 election that brought Conservative candidate Manuel A. Sanclamente to power and took up arms against the government. The war proved to be the bloodiest of Colombia's many civil conflicts, with as many as 100,000 killed. By the end of 1902, with the country's economy virtually paralyzed and government forces holding the military advantage, the Liberals agreed to surrender in return for amnesty.

The same year saw the Conservative government agree to the Hay-Herrán Treaty that gave the United States the rights to build a transoceanic canal across the Colombian province of Panama. But in 1903, the Colombian Senate unanimously refused to ratify the treaty on the grounds that U.S. control over the canal was incompatible with Colombian sovereignty. On November 3, 1903, Washington was presented with another opportunity to obtain the rights to build its canal when Panamanian secessionists revolted against Bogotá. President Theodore Roosevelt reacted to the uprising on the isthmus by dispatching U.S. warships and troops to prevent Colombian forces sent to quell the revolt from reaching Panama City.

Three days later Washington officially recognized Panamanian independence and signed a new treaty with Philip Buneau-Varilla—the former chief engineer of the Panama Canal Company and a member of the revolutionary *junta*—before legitimate representatives of the new Panamanian government could reach Washington. Roosevelt ignored Panama's protests regarding the canal treaty, which gave the U.S. jurisdiction over a canal zone that effectively cut the new country in half. Colombia also lodged official protests with Washington for supporting Panamanian independence, but was powerless to do anything about the situation.

While the loss of Panama caused many Colombians to resent and distrust the United States, some of the country's economic elite continued to push for expanded ties with their powerful northern neighbor. Political tensions between the two countries were partially alleviated in 1922 when the U.S. Senate ratified the Urrutia-Thompson Treaty that called for Washington to pay a $25 million indemnity to Colombia for the U.S. role in Panama's secession.

The ensuing years became known as the "Dance of the Millions," partly due to the $25 million payment, but primarily because Colombia's coffee production expanded dramatically and its banana, petroleum, and manufacturing sectors experienced significant growth. But the huge majority of Colombians were not benefiting from the country's booming economy, and rural and urban workers, often organized by local socialist and communist groups, began demanding social and economic reforms.

In the late 1920s, the emergence on the political scene of Jorge Eliécer Gaitán, a dissident Liberal Party member, offered hope to millions of impoverished and downtrodden Colombians. Gaitán first gained prominence with his public denunciations of the Conservative government's role in the Colombian army's 1928 massacre of striking banana workers in the northern town of Ciénaga, accusing the government and the army of being in the pocket of the Boston-based United Fruit Company. Gaitán was also instrumental in the labor and agrarian reform movements that in 1936 resulted in the introduction of Colombia's first modern agrarian reform law.[1]

Gaitán's populist rhetoric gained him a substantial following, and by the late 1940s, following a short stint as mayor of Bogotá, he was the presumed favorite to win the 1950 presidential election. On April 9, 1948, however, the Liberal leader was assassinated on a Bogotá street. Gaitán's death triggered the *Bogotazo*, a popular uprising by the Liberal lower classes that resulted in massive destruction and looting in the capital.

Many U.S. officials, including U.S. Secretary of State George C.

Marshall, who was attending the Ninth International Conference of American States in Bogotá when the violence broke out, believed the *Bogotazo* was part of a communist conspiracy to undermine the conference. According to Robert W. Drexler, who served as a U.S. diplomat in Colombia during the 1950s and again in the 1970s, "The rapidly growing obsession of the United States government with the Communist threat to Latin America can be dated from the *Bogotazo*, and it was a cruel irony of fate for Colombia that riots there arising from grave social ills led the United States to adopt militaristic anti-Communist policies in the area which generally ignored and sometimes even worsened those domestic problems."[2]

The rioting in Bogotá led to similar Liberal uprisings throughout the country in what became known as *La Violencia*. Fearing that the sporadic violence might coalesce into a peasant-based social revolution, the national Liberal leadership backed the bloody repression used by the Conservative government to quell it. Despite this loose alliance between the two parties, alleged Conservatives assassinated two high-ranking Liberals in 1949. In response, the Liberal Party boycotted the 1950 presidential election, which was won uncontested by Conservative candidate Laureano Gómez.

Although rebellion had been effectively suppressed in Bogotá, armed peasant uprisings continued throughout the countryside. The increasingly authoritarian Gómez regime—supported by the Catholic Church, a popular target of rebellious Liberal peasants during the uprisings—elevated the military crackdown to new heights, which only further fueled the violence. The chaotic conflict not only included battles between Liberal and Conservative peasants, but also between the oligarchy and land-starved peasants, leading many large landowners to abandon their properties for the relative safety of the cities. The United States, viewing Communist Party support for the peasants through a Cold War lens, rushed weapons and training to the Colombian military. Close military cooperation between the two countries had developed after Colombia became the only Latin American country to send combat troops to aid the U.S. war effort in Korea.

In 1952, a 23-year-old Argentine doctor named Ernesto "Che" Guevara arrived in Colombia after traveling throughout much of South America. During his brief stay, the man who would later inspire many Colombian revolutionaries noted, "There is more repression of individual freedom here than in any other country we've been to. . . . The atmosphere is tense and a revolution may be brewing."[3] High-ranking military officials also recognized the possible political and social implications of the rural violence and the inability of Gómez to quell it. In 1953, the Conservative president was ousted by a military coup that brought General Gustavo Rojas Pinilla to power.

Rojas Pinilla, the former commander of a Colombian infantry battalion in Korea, issued an amnesty to all armed peasants in an attempt to bring an end to *La Violencia*. While many peasants accepted the government's offer, others continued to fight. The dictator responded to the peasants' call for agrarian reform by creating the Office of Rehabilitation and Relief. In reality, this office did little to address the inequitable distribution of land, though it did make the Liberal and Conservative elite suspicious that Rojas Pinilla was using it to build popular support for himself.

In June 1954, Rojas Pinilla extended the amnesty to those who had been imprisoned for acts of terror on behalf of the Gómez regime. Many of these released *Gomezistas* quickly returned to killing Liberal peasants, forcing many of those who had accepted amnesty to once again take up arms in self-defense. In 1955, Rojas Pinilla responded to the new wave of violence by launching a major military offensive against armed Liberal and communist peasants in what came to be known as the War of Villarica.

The Conservative and Liberal elite blamed the renewed violence on Rojas Pinilla and, in 1957, organized a general strike and street protests in Bogotá that brought about the dictator's resignation. To fill the void, Conservatives and Liberals implemented a power sharing agreement called the National Front. Beginning in 1958, the two parties alternated four-year terms in the presidency and divided all government positions evenly between themselves. The National Front marked the end of the factional sparring between elites that had characterized Colombia's political violence from the nineteenth-century through *La Violencia*; however, the new unity government still had to contend with the armed peasants and gangs of marauding bandits.

Revolution's Call

Many Liberal and communist peasants survived the military offensives of the 1950s by undertaking long marches under the protection of armed self-defense movements to the mostly uninhabited departments of Meta and Caquetá in the vast Colombian Amazon. The peasants cleared and worked new lands in areas they declared "independent republics." However, these colonists did not find the autonomy they sought, as large landowners intent on increasing their own holdings began laying claim to the newly cleared areas. The national government, meanwhile, condemned the peasants as communist bandits and subjected them to an economic blockade. The Colombian military launched massive offensives against the independent republics, which included using U.S.-supplied B-26 bombers against peasant communities. The republics fell one by one, and once under government control, the land was usurped from the peasants and became concentrated in the hands of the large landowners.

Armed militants who were forced deeper into the jungle concluded that their only chance of achieving social justice lay in their ability to wage war against the government on a national level. The self-defense movements dispersed units to various regions of the country in order to fight the army on several fronts simultaneously. On July 20, 1964, the various fronts of the armed self-defense movements issued an agrarian reform program. Two years later the peasant rebels officially became the Revolutionary Armed Forces of Colombia (FARC)—which has become Colombia's largest guerrilla group.

Other guerrilla movements arose in the 1960s and 1970s as a challenge to the "limited democracy" of the National Front. The Cuban Revolution inspired radicals throughout Latin America, convincing many that Che Guevara's *foco* theory of armed insurrection was the revolutionary path to follow. Also, the Colombian Communist Party's support of resolutions passed by the Twentieth Soviet Congress in 1956, which called for a peaceful road to revolution, disappointed many young Colombians, leading them to break from the Party in order to follow the more radical Cuban model.

In 1964, university students in the northern department of Santander who had recently returned from Cuba formed what soon became the nation's second-largest guerrilla group, the National Liberation Army (ELN). In addition to Guevara, a key influence on the ELN was the Liberation Theology movement that evolved in part from the Catholic Church's Second Vatican Council call to place greater emphasis on the welfare of the poor. Many Latin

American priests incorporated Marxist ideology into their religious teachings and began calling for radical political, social, and economic reforms. One such Colombian priest, Camilo Torres Restrepo, joined the ELN in 1966, concluding that armed revolution was the only way to change the attitudes of the entrenched oligarchy. Although Torres was killed in his first military engagement, his example and writings influenced many leftists including a defrocked Spanish priest named Manuel Pérez Martinez, who joined the ELN in 1969. Fourteen years later, Pérez became the rebel group's commander-in-chief, a position he held until his death from hepatitis in 1998. Under Pérez's leadership the ELN did not become heavily involved in the drug trade, focusing instead on extortion and kidnapping to fund its insurgency.

The April 19 Movement (M-19) evolved out of the independent political party, the National Popular Alliance (ANAPO). In 1960, supporters of the deposed Rojas Pinilla formed ANAPO in order to participate in congressional elections. ANAPO's popularity increased steadily throughout the 1960s, finding support among those who had been left out of the National Front alliance. Rojas Pinilla ran as ANAPO's candidate in the 1970 presidential election and, after holding an early lead, was narrowly defeated by the National Front candidate, Misael Pastrana Borrero, in voting held on April 19. Many ANAPO supporters accused the government of manipulating the vote count, and, in response, some socialist members of the party formed the M-19 guerrilla group in 1972.

The M-19 gained notoriety through a series of daring urban raids, including the occupation of the Dominican Embassy in Bogotá in 1980 and the disastrous takeover of the Palace of Justice in 1985. The latter resulted in the deaths of more than one hundred people, including eleven Supreme Court justices, during a two-day battle in which the army shelled and leveled the massive courthouse in central Bogotá.[4] The M-19 never fully recovered from the Palace of Justice debacle, and in 1989 its members decided to lay down their weapons in return for a full government pardon. The ex-guerrillas formed a political party called the Democratic Alliance M-19 in order to participate in the upcoming elections; however, right-wing death squads assassinated many of the party's leaders, including presidential candidate and former M-19 commander Carlos Pizarro.

Of the guerrilla groups formed during the 1960s and early 1970s, the FARC alone has peasant roots that pre-date both the National Front and the Cuban Revolution. In contrast, the ELN and the M-19 were typical of the many leftist insurgencies that evolved throughout Latin America at the time—armed reactions to domestic political, social, and economic problems led by Cuban-inspired urban intellectuals.

Washington also responded to the threat the Cuban Revolution posed throughout the region. In order to counter the appeal of the Cuban example to millions of impoverished Latin Americans, the Kennedy administration developed a two-fold plan: intensifying the National Security Doctrine, a counterinsurgency strategy first formulated in 1946; and implementing development policies as part of a new program called the Alliance for Progress. Under the National Security Doctrine, Washington emphasized the training of Latin American militaries to fight internal rather than external enemies. This Cold War policy, which included the training of Colombian soldiers at the U.S. Army's School of the Americas, dramatically increased the levels of repression directed against domestic populations by U.S.-trained national militaries.

While the National Security Doctrine served as the stick in Washington's Latin America strategy, the carrot was the Alliance for Progress, which launched development and cultural projects throughout the region. Colombia was the first Latin American nation to initiate an Economic Development Plan under the Alliance, which was held up as a model of the U.S. program. However, Alliance for Progress projects that familiarized Colombians with U.S. culture and promoted economic development through a more humane form of capitalism did not result in dramatic structural changes. Washington only intended the Alliance to serve as a safety valve for releasing growing social pressures, while ensuring continued U.S. hegemony in the region.

The 1974 presidential election brought an end to the National Front as Liberal and Conservative candidates once again ran against each other. Sixteen years of National Front rule had reduced the amount of killings—in comparison to the 200,000 Colombians who died during *La Violencia*—but they failed to address the inequitable distribution of land and a dramatic increase in poverty. During the National Front years the percentage of the nation's work force living in absolute poverty more than doubled, from 25 percent to 50.7 percent. The figures were even worse for rural laborers, where the rate of absolute poverty soared from 25.4 percent to 67.5 percent.[5] With so many Colombians living under such dire conditions, it is no surprise that when the cocaine boom began in the late 1970s, the lure of drug profits resulted in a massive new migration of urban unemployed and landless peasants to the predominantly FARC-controlled regions to cultivate coca plants, which provide the raw ingredient for cocaine.

Initially, the FARC was concerned that this mass migration would undermine the political and social status quo in the areas it controlled. The FARC's mindset changed, however, when it saw that significant new revenue in the form of "war taxes" levied on the increasing local population would enable the rebel group to vastly improve its military capabilities by modernizing its weaponry and improving the standard of living of its fighters. In addition, the rebels were able to offer social and economic services, such as credit, public works, and cultural programs to the local peasantry.

The Proliferation of Paramilitaries

During the early years of the coca boom, the FARC worked in cooperation with the drug lords. The guerrillas controlled many of the coca-growing regions while the cartels in Medellín and Cali managed the cocaine production and trafficking. This informal alliance collapsed when the leaders of the cartels began investing their newfound wealth in property, primarily large cattle ranches, which placed them firmly in the ranks of the guerrillas' traditional enemies.

The guerrillas soon discovered another lucrative source of income: the kidnapping for ransom of narco-landowners and their relatives. In response to a spate of such kidnappings, drug traffickers in Cali organized a paramilitary group in order to combat the guerrillas and those they viewed as rebel sympathizers. Formed in December 1981, this militia was dubbed *Muerte a Secuestradores* (Death to Kidnappers, or MAS).

The next decade saw the establishment of hundreds of paramilitary organizations based on the MAS model. They were created, supported and funded by drug traffickers, large landowners, wealthy businessmen, and the Colombian military. Among those trained in 1981 for paramilitary duty by the Colombian army in Puerto Berrío, in the northwestern department of Antioquia, were Fidel and Carlos Castaño, two brothers whose father had been kidnapped and killed by the FARC. The brothers, who were also associates of the notorious Medellín drug cartel leader, Pablo Escobar, went on to form their own paramilitary force called the Peasant Self-Defense Groups of Córdoba and Urabá (ACCU). The ACCU soon became the largest and most feared militia in the country.

The Colombian army established another paramilitary organization in Puerto Boyacá, in the northern department of Santander, under the town's military mayor, Captain Oscar de Jesús Echandía. According to Human Rights Watch, "In 1982, Echandía convened a meeting of local people, including local Liberal and Conservative party leaders, businessmen, ranchers, and representatives from the Texas Petroleum Company. They found that their goal went far beyond protecting the population from guerrilla demands. They wanted to 'cleanse' (*limpiar*) the region of subversives."[6] Men were hired and armed in order to perform the "cleansing" with logistical support provided by the military. This new paramilitary force was named MAS, after the Cali organization.

On February 20, 1983, Colombia's attorney general released the results of an investigation ordered by President Belisario Betancur into death squad activity by MAS organizations. Of the 163 individuals implicated in the report, 59 were active members of the police or military. Father Javier Giraldo S.J., director of the Colombian human rights group Inter-Congregation of Peace and Justice, warned that the reaction of the armed forces and the minister of defense to the report seemed to indicate that a military coup was imminent. From that time on, the attorney general's office refrained from conducting serious investigations into paramilitary activities.[7]

On the rare occasion that a case against a member of the paramilitaries or the armed forces did make it to court, the judge, out of fear for his or her own life, would hand the case over to a military tribunal, which would then inevitably dismiss the charges. The military and paramilitary forces were able to wage war against suspected guerrilla sympathizers with impunity. Colombia, moreover, had spent most of the previous two decades under an official state of siege, during which the military had been given virtual autonomy in its handling of the civil conflict while the government focused almost exclusively on bureaucratic and administrative affairs. This dual system of government allowed the military and its paramilitary allies to function with little accountability or civilian oversight.

In 1985, following the signing of the La Uribe cease-fire accords between the FARC and President Betancur, the rebel group established a political party, the Patriotic Union (UP). As sociologist Ricardo Vargas points out, by addressing some of the FARC's socio-economic demands, "Betancur's position was a radical departure from that of his predecessors, for he recognized that guerrilla violence was the product of real social conditions and he understood the relationship between those conditions and the demands of the insurgents."[8]

Meanwhile, paramilitary organizations were undermining Betancur's peace process by intensifying their "dirty war" against suspected leftists, especially members of the Patriotic Union. Not only were many of the paramilitaries closely allied with the Colombian military, they were actually considered legal militias. In 1968, the passage of Law 48 permitted the military to organize and arm civilian "self-defense" units to fight against armed groups operating in certain peasant regions.[9] During the La Uribe peace talks, when counterinsurgency operations were prohibited, the army had intensified its application of Law 48 in order to create paramilitary forces capable of performing "cleansing" operations directed against the rural peasant population. The use of paramilitary forces in the dirty war during and after the cease-fire provided the military with a degree of plausible deniability with regard to human rights abuses.

Many legislators were opposed to Betancur's peace initiatives and, with the help of newly-elected President Virgilio Barco in 1986, quickly put an end to any negotiated threat to the interests of the oligarchy by ending the cease-fire. The Patriotic Union was decimated as right-wing death squads killed more than 2,000 members, including two presidential candidates and four elected congressmen, during the party's first five years.

Despite the proliferation of paramilitaries during the cease-fire, the FARC maintained control of many southern and eastern regions of the country, but in northern Colombia, paramilitary forces terrorized and displaced entire populations in order to implement an aggressive counter-agrarian reform campaign. These tactics allowed narco-landowners to increase the size of their land holdings, while at the same time disrupting bases of peasant support for the guerrillas. By the end of the 1980s, drug traffickers had become the largest landowners in the country and as a result had turned much of Colombia's arable land into unproductive cattle ranches.[10]

Although the military had been involved in the creation and operations of many paramilitary organizations, it did not always control them. By 1989, the narco-landowners were not only using their paramilitary forces against the guerrillas and peasants, they were also targeting government officials, especially politicians and judges who supported the extradition of drug traffickers to the United States or were critical of death-squad activities. On January 18, 1989, two judges and ten investigators looking into a number of killings by paramilitary forces were themselves massacred by paramilitaries. The death squads also targeted government officials they considered to be leftist sympathizers, especially former guerrillas. Carlos Castaño has admitted orchestrating the murder of former guerrilla leader and Democratic Alliance M-19 presidential candidate Carlos Pizarro. The paramilitary leader has also been sentenced in absentia to 22 years in prison by a Bogotá court for the 1990 killing of Patriotic Union presidential candidate Bernardo Jaramillo.

By the end of the 1980s, the government could no longer ignore the gruesome statistics: a dramatic increase in political killings from 1,053 victims per year in the 1970s to 12,859 in the 1980s.[11] President Virgilio Barco criticized the paramilitaries in an April 1989 address, stating, "The majority of their victims are not guerrillas. They are men, women and even children, who have not taken up arms against institutions. They are peaceful Colombians."[12] On May 25, the Colombian Supreme Court ruled that Law 48 was unconstitutional, and the following month President Barco issued Decree 1194, which made it illegal for civilians or members of the military to create, aid or participate in "self-defense" groups.

Outlawing the paramilitaries did little to diminish their activities or their affiliation with the armed forces. Human rights activist Father Giraldo describes the eyewitness account of an army informant present at the March 1990 Trujillo massacre, less than a year after the abolishment of Law 48 and the issuance of Decree 1194. "Just before midnight on the 31st, a combined army-paramilitary group dragged a large number of *campesinos* out of their houses, took them to the *hacienda* of a well-known drug trafficker and brutally tortured them, dismembering them with a chainsaw. The army major reserved the most brutal of the tortures for himself."[13]

When the Colombian courts failed to convict those accused of the massacre, Father Giraldo and his organization took the case to the Inter-American Commission of Human Rights at the Organization of American States on behalf of the 63 victims. After two years of discussions, the Colombian government agreed to create an extra-judicial commission consisting of governmental and non-governmental representatives. The newly formed Commission found the government responsible for the actions of the military personnel involved in the Trujillo massacre, and damages were awarded to the victims' families. However, because they had previously been absolved by the Colombian courts, those found responsible for the massacre were never punished.

During the 1990s, the FARC's upgrading of its military capabilities with revenues from coca taxes resulted in a corresponding increase in paramilitary activities, including massacres. By 1998 the FARC controlled 622 of the nation's 1,071 municipalities, up from only 173 in 1985.[14] While the rebel-controlled municipalities were primarily situated in sparsely populated rural regions of Colombia, they constituted some 40 percent of the national territory.

To combat the advances of the FARC, Carlos Castaño, who became leader of the ACCU following his brother's disappearance in 1994, expanded his paramilitary operations from the regional to the national level in April 1997. The resulting new organization, known as the United Self-Defense Forces of Colombia (AUC), was a coalition of paramilitary groups throughout the country. The AUC, which according to Castaño himself receives part of its income from narcotrafficking, then launched a military offensive against the guerrilla-controlled coca growing regions of southern Colombia.[15]

The AUC initiated its offensive in July 1997, when more than 100 paramilitaries massacred 49 peasants over a five-day period in the village of Mapiripán in southeastern Colombia. The weapons of choice for the paramilitary fighters were machetes and chainsaws, which they used to decapitate many of the victims. Government investigators later discovered that army troops had guarded the airstrip that the killers had used to enter and depart the rebel-dominated region. Colombian prosecutors formally accused Carlos

Castaño and Colombian army Colonel Lino Sánchez, commander of the U.S.-trained 2nd Mobile Brigade, of being the "intellectual authors" of the massacre.[16] The charges against Sánchez have since been dismissed, while Castaño remains at large with more than 22 warrants having been issued for his arrest over the past decade.

In February 2001, retired General Jaime Uscátegui, the army's regional commander at the time of the Mapiripán massacre, was sentenced by a military tribunal to 40 months in prison for failing to respond to calls to stop the slaughter. Even though Uscátegui was the first high-ranking Colombian military official ever to be convicted on charges relating to human rights abuses, human rights groups protested that the sentence was too lenient. In November 2001, Colombia's Constitutional Court ordered a retrial on the grounds that cases involving serious human rights violations should be heard by civilian courts.

U.S. Links to the Death Squads

In September 1989, President George Bush announced his Andean Initiative, which consisted of $2.2 billion of military and economic aid to Colombia, Peru and Bolivia. Two-thirds of the aid was earmarked for military and police units as part of the U.S. strategy of fighting the drug war on the military front while mostly ignoring rural poverty and the other economic causes of coca cultivation. While Washington overtly intensified its war against drugs, it also covertly became more involved in Colombia's counterinsurgency campaign. In 1990, Washington put together a fourteen-member team consisting of representatives from the U.S. Embassy's Military Group, U.S. Southern Command, the Defense Intelligence

Agency, and the CIA, to advise the Colombian military on a reorganization of its intelligence network. In May 1991, the intelligence reorganization was complete and the Colombian Defense Ministry issued Order 200-05/91. According to the stated objectives of the intelligence reorganization, the Order was supposed to address the drug trafficking problem. In actuality, there was no mention of drugs to be found in the 16-page Order. What was apparent in the Order was the U.S.-fostered formulation of a strategy to aid the Colombian military in its counterinsurgency war against the guerrillas.

One consequence of Order 200-05/91 was the undermining of Decree 1194, which had made it illegal for civilians and members of the military to create, aid, or participate in "self-defense" groups. Order 200-05/91 called for the military to create thirty intelligence networks and instructed local military commanders to "propose a list of candidates, whether civilians or retired military personnel, for integration into the networks' cadre."[17]

One of the thirty networks was created by the Colombian navy in Barrancabermeja, situated on the Magdalena River and the site of Colombia's largest oil refinery. A civilian member of that network, Felipe Gómez, admitted organizing several paramilitary groups at the military's behest. He also claimed to have "received weapons and equipment from the navy, including bolt-action rifles, M-16 rifles, Galil rifles, revolvers, pistols, submachine guns, fragmentation grenades, military instruction texts, and high-frequency two-way radios to communicate with the navy and the army."[18] Not only is it against Colombian law for civilians to possess many of these weapons, it is also, as a result of the 1989 Colombian Supreme Court decision that ruled Law 48 unconstitutional, illegal for the military to supply such arms to the civilian population.

Carlos David López, the Barrancabermeja intelligence network administrator, also testified to civilian authorities, and in his confession he attributed 46 murders to the network during the first six months of 1992.[19] Gómez, López, and other witnesses who testified about the Barrancabermeja intelligence network have since "disappeared."

The role of the paramilitaries was further legitimized on December 13, 1994, when President Ernesto Samper initiated a program called Cooperatives for Surveillance and Private Security (CONVIVIR). While the stated intent of this program was to allow armed civilians to establish rural security cooperatives for the purpose of providing the Colombian military with intelligence information, CONVIVIR groups were essentially paramilitary organizations. CONVIVIRs were finally outlawed in 1999 after many of them were implicated in human rights abuses, including massacres of civilians.

The reorganization of the Colombian Armed Forces' intelligence network is only one aspect of U.S. involvement in the Colombian military's dirty war. International human rights organizations claim that substantial amounts of U.S. aid in the 1990s went to Colombian army units with a history of human rights abuses and whose primary function was (and continues to be) fighting guerrillas, not the drug war. Even though the United States suspended military aid to Colombia from 1994 until 1997—in response to incessant human rights abuses and the revelation of President Ernesto Samper's connections to Cali narcotraffickers—there were 28 deployments of U.S. Special Forces to Colombia during 1996. These occurred under a 1991 U.S. law allowing military personnel to train on foreign soil if the purpose of the training is primarily to benefit U.S. troops.[20]

Even after aid was restored, the Clinton administration continued to utilize this 1991 law because it was not subject to the 1997 Leahy Amendment of the Foreign Operations Appropriations Act.

Under the Leahy Amendment, only Colombian military units cleared of human rights abuses are allowed to receive U.S. aid. These contradictory policies allowed the Clinton administration to publicly portray itself as a staunch defender of human rights without having to compromise its support for Colombia's repressive military forces.

Colombian officers and soldiers are also among the leading recipients of counterinsurgency training at the U.S. Army's Western Hemisphere Institute for Security Cooperation, formerly the School of the Americas (SOA), in Fort Benning, Georgia. According to Human Rights Watch, "Several of these officers were students at the school at the time its curriculum included training manuals recommending that soldiers use bribery, blackmail, threats, and torture against insurgents."[21]

Below is a partial list of notorious army officers among the more than 150 Colombian SOA graduates who have been linked by human rights organizations, the Colombian government, and even the U.S. State Department to human rights abuses and paramilitary death squads during the 1980s and 1990s:

• General Farouk Yanine Díaz—involved in the 1988 massacre of 20 banana workers in Urabá and the expansion of paramilitary death squads. Not only was Yanine Díaz a graduate of the SOA, but he also annually returned to the school as a guest speaker between 1986 and 1989.

• Major Luis Roberto García Ronderos—implicated in the 1988 massacre of 43 people, including several children, in the town of Segovia.

• Major Jorge Alberto Lazaro Vergel—arrested by the district attorney's office on charges that he directed the massacre of eight people in Puerto Patiño in 1995.

• Major Luis Fernando Madrid Barón—implicated in the activities of a paramilitary group that killed 149 people from 1987 to 1990. Madrid Barón was also accused of being the intellectual author of many of these assassinations.

• Major Carlos Enrique Martínez Orozco—implicated in the 1988 massacre of 18 miners in Antioquia. Martínez Orozco was subsequently promoted.

• Lieutenant Pedro Nei Acosta Gaivis—ordered the 1990 massacre of 11 peasants, then had his men dress the corpses to look like rebels and dismissed the killings as an armed confrontation between the army and guerrillas.

• Captain Humberto Sánchez Rey—implicated in the 1987 assassination of Patriotic Union presidential candidate, Jaime Pardo Leal.

• Colonel Jesús María Clavijo—currently under investigation for collusion with paramilitary forces in 160 social cleansing murders from 1995 to 1998.

• General Jaime Ernesto Canal Alban—established and supplied weapons and intelligence to a paramilitary group known as the Calima Front, which is responsible for more than 2,000 forced disappearances and at least 40 executions since 1999.

• General Carlos Ospina Ovalle—accused of maintaining extensive ties to paramilitary groups and whose troops massacred at least 11 people and burned down 47 homes in El Aro in 1998.

• General Mario Montoya Uribe—has a history of ties to paramilitary violence and is believed to be the military official responsible for Plan Colombia.

• Lieutenant Carlos Acosta—accused of executing a group of federal prosecutors and dumping their bodies in a river. According to Acosta's brother, "He used to say that a soldier in Colombia has to fight not only guerrillas, but also the human rights groups and prosecutors."[22]

In 2001, the SOA's name was changed to the Western Hemisphere Institute for Security Cooperation in an attempt to improve its public image, however, its mission remains the same: to train Latin American soldiers, not to defend their country against foreign aggressors, but to wage a domestic war against suspected subversives.

A family who was forcibly displaced by the civil conflict sits in front of their one-room wooden shack in San Vicente del Caguán, Caquetá.

One unfortunate *campesino*'s maize crop destroyed in Plan Colombia's initial fumigation campaign in the Guamuez Valley, Putumayo.

Photo: Garry M. Leech

A U.S.-supplied Colombian army Huey helicopter picks up troops from a base in La Hormiga, Putumayo, during an anti-guerrilla operation.

Photo: Garry M. Leech

Soldiers from a Colombian army anti-guerrilla unit patrol the streets in Doncello, Caquetá, near the border of the FARC safe-haven.

Traditionally dressed indigenous Guambiano women spinning yarn on market day in the central plaza in Silvia, Cauca.

Photo: Garry M. Leech

A Guambiano boy in the Andean highlands of Cauca tends to his sheep. The wool will be used by the tribe's women to weave their colorful clothing.

Photo: Garry M. Leech

Small garden plots of poppies, such as this, are a common sight behind the mud-brick houses of Guambiano families in the Andean highlands of Cauca.

AUC paramilitary fighters in the small village of La Dorada, Putumayo, wearing scarves to conceal their identities.

Photo: Garry M. Leech

A heavily armed National Police officer at a road blockade erected by peasants on the outskirts of Barrancabermeja, Santander, to protest the proposed safe-haven for the ELN.

Photo: Garry M. Leech

Colombia's innocuous-looking coca leaves provide the raw ingredient for 80 percent of the cocaine consumed in the United States.

Photo: Jason Howe

Colombian soldiers killed and wounded during the invasion of the former rebel safe-haven when a bus, booby trapped by the FARC, exploded on a highway in Caquetá.

Photo: Garry M. Leech

A *campesino* poses with his children and the prosthesis he received after losing his leg to a landmine planted on his farm in the rural zone of Zaragoza in northeastern Antioquia.

A FARC rebel patrol marching out of a camp situated deep in the jungle in Putumayo.

A *campesino* (right) in a hilltop courtroom near San Vicente del Caguán, Caquetá, presents his complaint to a FARC judge responsible for dispensing revolutionary justice.

The grisly sight of a body shoved halfway into a hole in the ground—one of 15 *campesinos* massacred three days earlier in the municipality of Los Angeles, Putumayo.

Graffiti in San Vicente del Caguán, Caquetá, comments on the country's dismal human rights situation: "In crazy-Colombia, there are neither rights nor humans."

PART TWO

Colombia and the New World Order

*He was weary of the uncertainty, of the
vicious circle of that internal war that always
found him in the same place, but always
older, wearier, even more in the position
of not knowing why, or how, or even when.*

Gabriel García Márquez
One Hundred Years of Solitude

Declaring War on Drugs

Washington has been battling drugs in the United States since the latter part of the nineteenth century, when it outlawed the use of opium. By the early twentieth century the targeted drug was marijuana, which was criminalized in 1937. However, it wasn't until the Nixon administration's escalation of the drug war in the 1970s that Washington began focusing primarily on source countries rather than on attempts to dissuade domestic users. During that decade, marijuana growers in the region around the Sierra Nevada de Santa Marta Mountains in northern Colombia became targets of aerial fumigation campaigns. By the end of the 1970s cocaine had replaced marijuana as Colombia's primary illegal drug export.

North America's seemingly insatiable appetite for cocaine allowed Pablo Escobar's Medellín drug cartel to evolve into a powerful and enormously wealthy criminal syndicate. Escobar gained popularity among impoverished Colombians, especially in Medellín, by building houses and schools in poor neighborhoods neglected by Colombian politicians. In 1982, Escobar's popularity with the lower classes led to his election as a Liberal Party alternate to the national Congress. But Escobar's foray into politics was short-lived, as the United States singled out the Medellín cartel as a target in its war on drugs. The Colombian government was pressured into issuing an arrest warrant for Escobar in September 1984. The drug lord responded by declaring war against the government and

launching a campaign of murder and intimidation against government officials.

What Escobar and his fellow traffickers most feared was extradition to the United States. In 1989, the Medellín leader and his associates escalated their violent campaign with the intention of forcing
the nation's political leaders into ending extradition and negotiating a peace agreement between the government and the traffickers.
The cartel's leaders, calling themselves the "Extraditables," launched
a wave of urban bombing that terrorized the nation. Between 1989
and 1993, some 40 car bombs killed more than 500 people, and the
1989 bombing of an Avianca airliner en route from Bogotá to Cali
killed 119 passengers.[1]

In 1991, Escobar reached an agreement with the Colombian
government that called for him to end the violence and cease all
drug trafficking activities in return for a lenient sentence to be
served in a custom-built Colombian prison. In July 1992, Escobar
fled his luxury prison igniting an enormous manhunt that resulted
in the assassination of many of his associates. For sixteen months,
U.S. intelligence agencies, Colombian law enforcement, and the
rival Cali cartel worked together to track down the leader of the
rapidly crumbling Medellín cartel. Finally, in December 1993, state
security forces gunned down Escobar on a Medellín rooftop. But
Colombia's narcotrafficking continued unabated.

The focus of U.S. drug warriors turned to the Cali cartel,
Colombia's new dominant narcotrafficking organization. Unlike
Escobar, Cali's leaders kept a low profile and used their drug profits
to discreetly buy influence with many of Colombia's politicians,
including former President Ernesto Samper. The Cali cartel's size
and the scope of its operations left it vulnerable, and, in the mid-
1990s, the cartel was essentially decapitated when many of its leaders were arrested. This drug war "victory" also failed to slow the

flow of drugs to the United States.

The demise of the Cali cartel resulted in a de-monopolization of the illicit drug industry, with hundreds of small cartels becoming involved in the Colombian drug trade. Unlike the Medellín and Cali cartels—which controlled much of the drug trade from cultivation to processing to trafficking to selling the finished product on the streets of U.S. cities—today's drug lords outsource many of their operations. They contract individuals to pick up the coca leaves or opium latex and deliver them to processing labs. They use independent "mules" and groups to ship the drugs northward, often to Mexico, where local gangs handle the distribution of cocaine and heroin to the United States. As a result, it has become much more difficult for Washington to infiltrate the new cartels.

Each victory over Colombia's drug traffickers has resulted in the emergence of new, more efficient, and obscure organizations. A similar sort of balloon effect (squeezing the drug trade in one place results in expansion elsewhere) was occurring simultaneously as a result of the "successful" coca eradication operations in Bolivia and Peru. Up until the mid-1990s, these two South American nations were the principal cultivators of coca. The Medellín and Cali cartels would purchase the raw coca leaves or paste from growers in Bolivia and Peru and transport them to Colombia for processing into cocaine. But by the end of the 1990s, U.S.-sponsored aerial fumigation campaigns had drastically reduced the amount of coca being cultivated in Bolivia and Peru. Nevertheless, the amount of coca being cultivated in South America remained at the same level as before the eradication campaigns. Coca cultivation had simply moved to Colombia, where it doubled between 1995 and 2000.[2]

The eradication campaigns in Bolivia and Peru have actually made life easier for drug traffickers, who no longer have to transport raw coca leaves through remote jungles and across rugged mountains to their Colombian processing labs. And yet, Washington insists on pointing to the "success" of the campaigns in Bolivia and Peru as an example of what it can achieve in Colombia.

The increased coca cultivation in rural Colombia has provided massive amounts of funding to leftist guerrillas and right-wing paramilitaries, who tax all growers and traffickers in the regions under their control. As a result, the illegal armed groups have dramatically bolstered their military strength as Colombia's civil conflict has become increasingly fueled by profits from the drug trade.

Colombia's Economic Crisis

Colombians from all walks of life have been victimized by the escalating violence, but for the 55 percent of the population living in poverty, brutality in the form of economic globalization is exacerbating the miserable conditions under which they are forced to endure life. In 1999, the relatively stable Colombian economy sank into its worst recession in more than half a century as the nation's unemployment rate climbed to almost 20 percent, the highest in Latin America. In December 1999, in a desperate attempt to stimulate the economy, the government agreed to a $2.7 billion loan from the International Monetary Fund (IMF).

While the endemic violence is partially responsible for Colombia's economic decline, it is not the principal cause. After all, the intensity of the conflict during *La Violencia* far exceeded that experienced during the 1990s, and yet the economy displayed impressive growth during the late 1940s and 1950s. What did occur during the past decade was *la apertura*—"the opening." In September 1989, U.S. President George Bush announced the $2.2

billion Andean Initiative, in part to help Colombia combat the urban bombing campaign being carried out by drug traffickers. The following month, Bush welcomed Colombian President Virgilio Barco to Washington to discuss trade initiatives for the Andean region. In a statement afterwards, Bush said the United States "aims to encourage and support fundamental economic reform in the countries of the region on the basis of market-driven policies."[3]

The following year, Colombia's newly elected president, César Gaviria launched *la apertura*, which implemented the "market-driven policies" called for by President Bush. These neoliberal policies opened up Colombia's economy to an increased flow of foreign investment and goods.

World Bank statistics show that between 1989 and 1993, Colombia's average tariff decreased from 44 percent to less than 12 percent, resulting in lower prices for imported goods. Consequently, the country's trade surplus soon became a trade deficit. In 1989, Colombian exports totaled $7.3 billion and imports $6.4 billion—a surplus of almost one billion dollars. But only nine years later, exports of $13.6 billion were surpassed by imports totaling $17.5 billion, resulting in a deficit of close to $4 billion.[4] It soon became apparent that the government's policies were negatively impacting domestic producers who were unable to compete with the high-tech industries of scale in developed countries.

As a result of lower tariffs, the amount of government revenue earned from import taxes declined, as did the tax revenue gained from small and medium-sized domestic companies, many of which had gone out of business. A further loss of revenue has resulted from the former employees of these now-defunct companies being unemployed or working in the informal sector and, therefore, no longer paying income taxes. While government revenue was declining throughout the 1990s, expenditures increased. This fiscal imbal-

ance became unmanageable when, in 1999, the Colombian economy experienced its worst year since the Great Depression. It took
longer than most other Latin American countries, but Colombia
finally reached the point of economic desperation that provides the
IMF with the leverage it needs to impose economic policies that
benefit multinational corporations.

The adjustment conditions laid out in the $2.7 billion IMF loan
require Colombia to further open its economy, privatize public
companies, and cut social spending, bringing Colombia into the
fold of the U.S-dominated new world economic order. The IMF's
policies demand that Colombia, despite financial hardships resulting
from the civil conflict and economic recession, reduce its budget
deficit in order to make funds available for foreign debt payments.
These policies stand in sharp contrast to Washington's defense of its
own budget deficits during times of crisis.[5]

In all likelihood, as occurred during the 1990s, a further opening of the Colombian economy will continue to reduce government revenue, hurt both small and medium-sized businesses, and
eliminate—not create—jobs. The privatization of state-owned entities, such as banks, utilities, and mining companies, will be a bonan-
za for those who can afford to purchase them—namely, multinational corporations and Colombia's economic elite, which is comprised of five huge conglomerates that dominate the nation's industrial sector and own virtually all the major media outlets. But this
privatization process will likely result in massive lay-offs as private
investors streamline operations in order to maximize profits with
little regard for the public's welfare. Due to the public spending cuts
required under the terms of the IMF loan agreement, the government will be unable to cope with the inevitable increases in unemployment and poverty.

Still, the globalization process in Colombia has met some obstacles, namely the guerrillas, trade unions, and the Colombian courts. In September 2000, the sale of the city-owned Bogotá Telecommunications Company (ETB) was abandoned after potential Spanish and Italian buyers pulled out of the deal due to increased guerrilla kidnappings and violence. Bogotá authorities have valued ETB—Latin America's largest remaining government-owned telecommunications company—at $1.4 billion. However, ETB union leaders claim the company's true value is closer to $5 billion. ETB made a $69 million profit even in the folds of the economic crisis of 1999 and already has the capacity to double the number of phone lines it presently provides. If the sale had gone through, the city of Bogotá would have walked away with $710 million in profit.[6] But by retaining ownership of ETB, Bogotá should earn that amount in approximately ten years, and everything it garners thereafter will be additional profit.

Also in September 2000, Colombia's Constitutional Court suspended the sale of the nation's second-largest electric company, state-owned Isagen, after another Colombian utility, the Medellín Public Company, complained it had been unfairly excluded from a bidding process that favored multinational corporations. A few years earlier, the Colombian government had attempted to sell another state-owned electric company, Interconexion Eléctrica (ISA), along with Isagen. However, the privatization of ISA was repeatedly suspended because of rebel attacks against its installations. Guerrilla attacks damaged hydroelectric stations and destroyed more than 360 electricity towers in the 18 months prior to September 2000, which made ISA a tough sell. As a result, the Colombian government continues to collect the profits made by both Isagen and ISA. Isagen posted a $2 million profit in 2000, while ISA pocketed $60 million in profits during the first nine months of 2001.[7]

Why is the Colombian government so eager to unload these

revenue-producing entities? It has no choice. The government must abide by the IMF's stringent demands or face a political and economic backlash from the international lending institutions, multinational corporations and the governments of developed nations, especially the United States. As Joseph E. Stiglitz, Nobel Laureate and former chief economist at the World Bank, explains, "The mandate [of the IMF] often appears to be that of a bill collector for lending nations: its objective is to make sure that the debtor country has as large a war chest as possible to repay outstanding loans."[8]

In the long-term, ETB, Isagen, and ISA will provide the Colombian government with revenues far greater than the one-off amounts it can potentially earn through their sale. Moreover, once Colombia loses these sources of revenue it will most likely be forced to seek another IMF bailout. Colombia's auditor general Carlos Ossa has tried in vain to convince the government to resist the IMF-mandated privatization of the country's electric companies. Ossa argues that there is no reason to sell profitable state-owned utilities.[9] But advocates of privatization claim private corporations will operate these companies more efficiently and the greater profits earned will result in increased tax revenues for the government. However, they neglect to consider that, historically, foreign corporations operating in Latin America benefit from corrupt political systems that offer them incredibly generous tax exemptions, which inevitably result in most of the profits leaving the country.

It is not always easy to collect taxes from multinational corporations, a fact illustrated by a suit filed by 24 of Colombia's departmental governments and the capital district of Bogotá in U.S. Federal Court in September 2000. They claim that the world's second-largest cigarette manufacturer, British American Tobacco (BAT)—maker of the Kool and Kent brands—has defrauded

Colombia of tax and other revenues. The suit is similar to one filed in May 2000 against Philip Morris, charging the maker of Marlboro cigarettes with racketeering, smuggling, and money laundering activities that defrauded the Colombian government of billions of dollars in revenue.

The multinational tobacco companies have avoided paying the Colombian government import taxes by illegally moving cigarettes into the country using centuries-old smuggling routes in the north-eastern department of La Guajira. A six-month investigation carried out by independnet journalist Mark Schapiro recently demonstrated how massive advertising campaigns and cheap blackmarket prices led to the market share for imported cigarettes in Colombia skyrocketing from 15 percent in 1984 to 70 percent in 1993. As a result, Schapiro explains, "Since 1984 the amount of hectares devoted to tobacco crops in Colombia has plummeted. As the domestic cigarette industry imploded, many tobacco farmers made the shift to Colombia's far more famous addictive crop, coca."[10]

Not only has the smuggling of cigarettes by multinational manufacturers contributed to increased coca cultivation, it has also helped drug traffickers launder their dirty money through the Black Market Peso Exchange (BMPE). The BMPE launders illicit funds through the purchasing of foreign goods, such as electronic appliances, cigarettes, or other luxury items, with dollars earned from drug trafficking. Those goods are then smuggled into Colombia where they are sold for pesos. Colombian traffickers often take a loss on the exchange, but simply write it off as the cost of laundering narco-dollars into pesos. Meanwhile, the multinational corporations whose products are purchased with drug dollars, the smugglers, and the Colombian retailers all profit from the BMPE while domestic producers in Colombia are unable to compete with the cheap illegal imports.

The money-laundering and fraud charges against Philip Morris and BAT stem not only from claims that some of their cigarettes are purchased with narco-dollars, but that the manufacturers are actually orchestrating smuggling operations that have flooded Colombia with illegal cigarettes. In 1992, according to the U.S. Department of Agriculture, $21.6 million worth of cigarettes were exported from the United States to Colombia. But the Colombian Department of National Statistics (DANE), reports that only $10.7 million worth were legally imported into Colombia during that year.[11] According to Alex Solognier, former chief financial officer for BAT's Colombian distributor, "They [BAT] knew that all these cigarettes were being smuggled."[12]

In all likelihood, the multinational cigarette manufacturers will not have to rely on their underground globalization tactics for much longer. If future IMF-imposed austerity measures result in the Colombian government lowering the tariffs placed on imported cigarettes, then Philip Morris and BAT will be able to complete the process of eliminating domestic competition and ensuring their domination of Colombia's cigarette market through legal channels.

The globalization process is also undermining Colombia's traditionally stable coffee economy. For many years, the cultivation of coffee beans provided farmers in the coffee-growing areas a measure of security and stability in the midst of Colombia's violence. But the international market price for coffee—Colombia's third-largest legal export, behind oil and coal—has plummeted in the past year, forcing many farmers to seek alternative means of survival. Increasing numbers of coffee growers have begun replacing their coffee plants with coca bushes. Those in the higher elevations of the Andes have turned to raising opium poppies, the principal raw ingredient for heroin. While cultivating drug crops has enabled farmers to survive, it has also brought the guerrillas and paramilitaries into the coffee-growing regions, escalating the violence and expanding the reach of the various armed groups.

The dilemma now faced by Colombia's coffee growers began with a World Bank development project in Vietnam that, during the 1990s, encouraged Vietnamese farmers to grow coffee. The program was so "successful" that in 2001 Vietnam surpassed Colombia to become the number two coffee producing country in the world behind Brazil. However, a resulting global glut in coffee caused the market price to plummet from over $2 a pound at the end of the 1980s to 58 cents by the end of 2001. Consequently, coffee growers around the world, including those in Vietnam, are now desperately struggling to survive by growing a crop that sells for less than it costs to produce.

In the meantime, the declining cost of coffee has not been reflected at the retail end of the equation. The multinational coffee corporations are the ones reaping the benefits of the World Bank's Vietnam project. By keeping retail prices constant while the cost of coffee beans was plummeting, corporations increased their earnings dramatically. In fact, Starbucks reported a record profit of $181.2 million in 2001, a 92 percent increase over the previous year.[13] Ironically, the United States—the key player in the World Bank— has indirectly undermined its drug war efforts in Colombia by forcing coffee growers to turn to illicit crop cultivation in order to survive. But this consequence may be of secondary concern to Washington politicians who are pledged to protect the interests of U.S. corporations such as Starbucks and Kraft Foods (owner of the Maxwell House brand).

The IMF-imposed austerity measures, which favor foreign debt payments over agricultural subsidies, severely restrict the Colombian government's options for helping struggling coffee growers. This highlights the hypocrisy prevalent in Washington's so-called "free trade" agenda. Neoliberal policies force farmers in developing nations to compete in the global marketplace without government protection, while U.S. and European farmers continue to benefit from substantial state subsidies that violate the primary tenet of free trade.

In June 2001, tens of thousands of Colombians took to the streets in several cities to protest government budget cuts mandated by the IMF. Teachers, health workers and students claimed the proposed tax reforms would adversely affect health and education funding by allowing the government to avoid its constitutional obligation to transfer half of its income to regional authorities. Instead, the government intends to use the money to service the foreign debt in order to meet its IMF obligations.

As a result of neoliberal economic policies, many marginalized Colombians have turned to the armed groups, the drug trade, or street crime as alternative means of survival. This has escalated the armed conflict and resulted in high levels of criminal violence. In March 2002, even Colombia's labor minister, Angelino Garzón, admitted that the policies of the IMF "have contributed to the impoverishment of large sectors of the population."[14]

The Dirty War

Millions of peasants have been caught in the middle of a conflict between armed actors that refuse to recognize any declarations of neutrality by rural communities. The Colombian army and its paramilitary allies often accuse rural Colombians of having leftist sympathies, while the FARC and ELN in turn accuse them of rightist leanings. Every year thousands of *campesinos* are killed, kidnapped or forcibly displaced from their homes by one or more of these groups.

In the past decade, more than 40,000 Colombians have been killed in the civil conflict. Paramilitary groups, often supported by the Colombian military, are responsible for 78 percent of the country's human rights violations, including most of the nation's massacres.[15] Human Rights Watch detailed one gruesome episode during which 300 paramilitaries entered the village of El Salado, in the northern department of Bolívar, on February 18, 2000, and "tortured, garroted, stabbed, decapitated, and shot residents. Witnesses told investigators that they tied one six-year-old girl to a pole and suffocated her with a plastic bag. One woman was reportedly gang-raped. Authorities later confirmed thirty-six dead. Thirty other villagers were missing."[16] During the carnage, the Colombian navy's First Brigade erected roadblocks outside El Salado, effectively denying the International Red Cross access to the village. Not until 30 minutes after the paramilitaries had left did naval forces enter the village.[17]

Similar massacres continued throughout 2001, with the largest occurring on October 10 in the tiny village of Alaska, near Buga, in the Valle de Cauca. On that fateful day, some 30 paramilitaries entered the village in the early afternoon and initiated a killing spree that left 24 peasants dead, including three children.

Paramilitary forces are also responsible for much of the displacement, especially in northern Colombia where many peasants have been forced to abandon lands in areas possessing valuable natural resources such as oil, coal, gold, and emeralds. By the end of 1999, just three percent of landowners had amassed ownership of more than 70 percent of the country's arable land.[18]

During the past decade, more than two million Colombians have fled their homes because of the ongoing violence, resulting in the third-largest internally displaced population in the world after the

Sudan and Angola. According to the Colombian Human Rights and Displacement Consultancy (CODHES), some 341,925 Colombians were forcibly displaced by violence in 2001, an average of 39 people each hour.[19]

In November 2000, the entire village of La Ciénaga, southern Bolívar, fled to the relative safety of Barrancabermeja in the northern department of Santander. The exodus was triggered when, according to one villager, Luis Hernández, paramilitaries came to La Ciénaga and killed several residents, including two of his friends. Afraid they would return, the 130 villagers—more than half of them children—abandoned their homes and settled into cramped and unfamiliar urban surroundings. The paramilitaries continued to threaten them in Barrancabermeja, forcing one of their leaders to flee the city.[20]

While men are more likely to be the victims of massacres, it is women and children who constitute a disproportionate percentage of the displaced population. In 1999 alone, 176,800 children were forced from their homes by violence. According to Claudia Marcela Barona of UNICEF in Bogotá, children constitute 65 percent of Colombia's displaced population.[21] Most of Colombia's displaced end up living in poverty-ridden shantytowns that are rapidly encircling the country's cities. The impoverished residents of these communities rarely have access to electricity, water or waste disposal. Many of the children are forced to abandon school in order to help support their struggling families. Inevitably, some of these children wind up on the streets as prostitutes or petty criminals. According to María Eugenia Martínez of the Youth Service Foundation, a Colombian non-governmental organization that works with street children, there are between 12,000 and 13,000 people living on the streets of Bogotá, and more than 40 percent of them are children and adolescents.[22]

The country's middle and upper classes have also been victimized by the civil conflict. Colombia leads the world in kidnappings—with 3,706 abductions in 2000 alone.[23] The FARC and the ELN hold middle- and upper-class Colombians for ransom in order to fund their insurgencies and are responsible for the majority of abductions committed by the armed groups. In March 2000, the FARC issued its Law 002, which demands that every person or corporation worth at least one million dollars pay a "peace tax" to the rebels. Those who do not, says the FARC, will be detained and "their liberation shall depend upon the payment of the determined sum."[24]

The guerrillas are also primarily responsible for a majority of the estimated 100,000 anti-personnel mines that are scattered throughout the Colombian countryside. Landmines are present in at least 168 municipalities in 24 of Colombia's 32 departments. While the Colombian government is a signatory to the 1997 Ottawa Convention's Mine Ban Treaty, which prohibits the use, production, or stockpiling of anti-personnel landmines, the Colombian military has yet to remove any of the 20,000 mines it laid prior to 1998. For their part, the guerrillas, and to a lesser extent the paramilitaries, continue to utilize anti-personnel mines in populated areas. In 2001, of the 203 known landmine victims, 51 were killed while 152 were permanently disabled. More than half of the victims were civilians, and the majority of those were children.[25]

The residents of the rural zone of Zaragoza, in northeastern Antioquia, have had to endure the threat of landmines for many years. In the past three years alone there have been 11 victims of mines and unexploded ordnance. On September 9, 2000, Jorge Eliécer Rodríguez stepped on a landmine beside a dirt path on his farm. According to Jorge, "I felt the explosion and then fell. . . . It blew my foot off. I tried to jump on my only good leg, but I fainted." By the time his relatives got him to the nearest hospital in this remote rural region it was too late to save his left leg. Despite now being dependent on his wife to operate the family's small farm, Jorge and his family have refused to join the ranks of Colombia's rapidly growing displaced rural population by fleeing to the relative safety of the city. But Jorge's wife, Aniana Sierra, worries about their three young children, "They can't go far from the house because we don't know if there are more mines. We have notified the army, but they say they don't have mine detectors."[26] The Rodríguez family and millions of other rural Colombians continually live in fear of these indiscriminate killers.

The illegal armed groups, intent on controlling mineral-rich indigenous lands, have also targeted Colombia's indigenous communities. During 2001, more than 300 Indians were killed by guerrillas and paramilitaries, both of which, says Armando Valbuena, president of the National Indigenous Organization of Colombia (ONIC), "have become enemies and oppressors of Indian populations."[27] The Colombian army has also persecuted Colombia's indigenous peoples, especially the U'wa in the department of Norte de Santander. On February 11, 2000, three U'wa children were killed during a confrontation between unarmed indigenous protesters and the army, which has served as protector of exploration and drilling operations being conducted by the Los Angeles-based Occidental Petroleum Corporation. The Colombian army's role in protecting the interests of Occidental is eerily reminiscent of its 1928 massacre of striking United Fruit workers in Ciénaga.

The conflict between Occidental and the U'wa escalated when the Ministry of the Environment definitively redrew the boundaries of the U'wa territory. The government strategically left outside the reservation a piece of land that had traditionally belonged to the tribe but which Occidental and its former partner in the venture,

Royal Dutch Shell, coveted. The Ministry of the Environment also happens to be the government department responsible for handing out concessions to corporations interested in exploiting Colombia's natural resources, including oil.

When the U'wa protested the newly drawn property lines, the government offered them two other small pieces of land that adjoined their territory. The U'wa rejected the offer, citing the importance of the Cubogon River, which runs through the land that includes the Occidental drilling site. The Cubogon is the principal river in U'wa territory, and the tribe is concerned about possible environmental damage and the oil access roads that will result in a new wave of colonization in the region. The oil camp is located only 150 feet from the river, and if the history of Occidental's Caño Limón-Coveñas pipeline in the department of Arauca is any indication, it will inevitably become an environmental hazard. Guerrilla forces have attacked the Caño Limón-Coveñas pipeline more than 700 times since 1986, spilling more than 1.7 million barrels of oil into Colombia's fragile ecosystem.[28]

Under Colombia's 1991 Constitution, any corporation planning to work in the vicinity of indigenous lands, or whose activities will affect indigenous people or their lands, must seek approval from the local indigenous community. According to U'wa representative Ebaristo Tegria Uncaria, Occidental failed to discuss its oil exploration and drilling plans with the tribe.[29]

In his February 2000 testimony to the United States Congress in support of the Clinton administration's $1.3 billion aid package for Colombia, Occidental vice-president Lawrence P. Meriage used red-baiting, Cold War language to associate non-governmental organizations (NGOs) with Marxist insurgents. "Only two groups are intent on blocking [Occidental's oil exploration]—leftist guerrillas who seek to undermine the country's democratically elected government and several fringe non-governmental organizations in the United States. Both groups are united in their opposition to oil exploration and development."[30]

Such irresponsible linking of NGOs with guerrilla groups has endangered the lives of many indigenous, labor and human rights activists in a country where right-wing paramilitaries have repeatedly targeted NGO workers. Meriage's simplistic analysis failed to note that right-wing paramilitaries sympathetic to Occidental's economic interests have attacked and threatened to kill several U'wa representatives, including the tribe's leader, Roberto Cobaria. Also, Meriage's claim that leftist guerrillas and NGOs are "united" fails to explain why the FARC kidnapped and killed three U.S. activists working with the U'wa in 1999.

Colombia's most intense urban warfare has been waged in Barrancabermeja (known locally as Barranca), located on the Magdelana River and home to the country's largest oil refinery. In December 2000, paramilitary forces launched an urban offensive against the ELN and the FARC targeting not only guerrillas, but also human rights workers, trade unionists, and local civic groups. Prior to the offensive, Carlos Castaño announced that he wanted this oil-rich port city of 200,000 cleansed of guerrillas. Battles erupted between paramilitaries and rebels in the streets of Barranca's poor neighborhoods as the AUC methodically seized barrio after barrio until it controlled much of the city. AUC forces have repeatedly kidnapped suspected rebel sympathizers from their homes in the middle of the night. On most occasions the abducted simply "disappear," although a corpse occasionally turns up.

Over the past decade Barranca has averaged 330 murders a year, but according to Régulo Madero Fernández, local president of the Regional Corporation for the Defense of Human Rights (CRED-HOS), in recent years the death rate has risen dramatically, with 567 politically motivated murders in the year 2000.[31] The paramilitaries have been responsible for many of the killings, but they have not implemented this dirty war alone. The few police present in para-military-controlled neighborhoods make no attempt to confront members of the AUC who openly patrol the streets with mobile phones, walkie-talkies and 9mm pistols tucked conspicuously in their waistbands.

According to Mateo, a young FARC guerrilla in Barrio Boston, "The paramilitaries receive a lot of support from the public forces. When there is a problem in Simon Bolívar or Miraflores, the police do nothing. But if there is a problem in a guerrilla neighborhood, they launch an operation."[32] Madero echoes Mateo's claims of col-laboration between government forces and the paramilitaries. "The complicity between the institution of the government, the public forces and the paramilitaries is a fact. These things generate an anar-chic situation and the first victims are human rights and the digni-ty of the people."[33]

A local AUC leader known as Javier blames the guerrillas for Barranca's problems. "The people know that the guerrillas have been the government in Barrancabermeja for a long time and have seen the things those bandits are doing. It's not good what they are doing. They don't bring anything good for us." Javier lives in the neighborhood known as Comuna 7 and claims to be "worried about defending the people because human rights have not existed here."[34] According to one human rights organization, however, it is the paramilitaries who have "targeted the population of Comuna 7, calling mandatory meetings, forcing residents to sign statements in opposition to community organizations, and threatening all those who don't comply."[35]

Colombia is the most dangerous country in the world in which to campaign for labor rights. One hundred and eighty-four union activists were murdered in 2001, while at least 1,600 Colombian union members have received death threats in the past three years. Also in 2001, according to the International Confederation of Free Trade Unions, the AUC named 104 specific unionists as military targets because they were, the paramilitaries claimed, "puppets of the guerrilla forces and traitors to the country."[36]

In total, more than 3,000 unionists have been assassinated in the past 15 years without a single culprit being convicted. This outrage has recently led Colombian unions to file suits in U.S. courts accusing two U.S. companies operating in Colombia—Coca-Cola and Drummond Mining—of maintaining links to paramilitary death squads responsible for the killings of labor leaders.

In the Coca-Cola case, a lawsuit filed on July 20, 2001, in U.S. District Court in Florida, accuses Coca-Cola, its Colombian subsidiary and business affiliates of using paramilitary death squads to murder, torture, kidnap and threaten union leaders at the multinational soft drink manufacturer's Colombian bottling plants. On December 5, 1996, Isidro Segundo Gil, executive board member of Sinaltrainal—the union that represents Coca-Cola bottlers in Colombia—was killed by paramilitaries at the entrance to the Carepa bottling plant. Two and a half months earlier, the union had sent a letter to Coca-Cola Colombia informing them of threats made against the union by the plant manager and requesting that the company intervene to prevent human rights abuses against employees and union leaders. Coca-Cola failed to respond to the request.

Sintramienergetica, the union that represents Alabama-based Drummond Mining's Colombian workers, filed a similar suit in U.S. Federal Court in Alabama on March 14, 2002, accusing Drummond's Colombian managers of using paramilitaries to kill three union leaders. The suit was filed one year and two days after a company bus taking workers to Drummond's Loma mine in northern Colombia was stopped by a paramilitary death squad. Valmore Locarno Rodríguez and Víctor Hugo Orcasita, the chairman and vice-chairman of the mine's union, were removed from the bus and executed by the gunmen. Drummond had recently denied a request by the union leaders that they be allowed to sleep at the mine because of paramilitary threats. On October 6, the new chairman of the union, Gustavo Soler Mora, was also murdered by paramilitaries.

The killings of Colombian unionists by right-wing paramilitaries allied with the Colombian military has caused U.S. labor leader Leo Gerard, president of the United Steel Workers, to openly criticize Washington's support for Colombia's armed forces. "We are strongly opposed to the amount of military aid being sent to the Colombian army when unionists and innocent people are being killed by the very military forces we are financing."[37]

Another tragic aspect of the conflict has been the dramatic increase in "social cleansing" killings committed by right-wing death squads. The mission of many paramilitary organizations now includes the elimination of drug addicts, petty thieves, prostitutes, homosexuals, beggars, and street children. In 1996, according to the Colombian government's Institute of Legal Medicine and Forensic Sciences, more than 2,000 people were killed as a result of social cleansing performed by death squads or assassins known as *sicarios*.[38] Many of these *sicarios* come from the ranks of the young urban unemployed who are becoming increasingly marginalized as a result of Colombia's deteriorating economy. Once their employers decide they know too much, these young assassins often become the targets of newly recruited *sicarios*.

Colombia also holds the ignominious title as the most deadly country in the world for members of the press. In 2001, according to the Paris-based World Association of Newspapers (WAN), ten journalists were killed in Colombia, bringing the total to 31 since 1997. In addition to the killings, dozens of reporters have been kidnapped and more than 100 have fled into exile. The New York-based Committee to Protect Journalists (CPJ) blames both sides for the persecution of Colombian reporters, claiming that "right-wing paramilitaries were the worst offenders, but journalists had plenty to fear from leftist guerrilla organizations as well."[39]

The violence in Colombia has tragically affected virtually every segment of society. The armed combatants constitute only a small number of the casualties in a conflict whose victims have overwhelmingly been innocent civilians.

A Plan for Corporate America

In the 1980s, the Reagan administration introduced the terms "narco-guerrilla" and "narco-terrorist" as a means of demonizing leftist insurgent groups around the world by linking them to international drug trafficking. During the 1990s, the Clinton administration applied the Reagan-era rhetoric to Colombia by repeatedly labeling the FARC as "narco-guerrillas" in order to justify further militarizing the war on drugs. In so doing, Washington has seriously misrepresented a civil conflict that has, for more than fifty years, been deeply rooted in Colombia's political, social, and economic inequalities.

Washington's insistence on an overseas military solution to its domestic drug problem has drawn the United States into Colombia's civil conflict. In 1998, the U.S. Congress allocated $290 million in anti-drug aid to Colombia to be spent over three years.

The huge majority of this money was earmarked for the purchase of U.S.-made helicopters and weaponry for military and police use in coca eradication campaigns. Only $45 million of the aid went for crop substitution programs aimed at replacing illicit crops with legal ones. However, despite Washington's efforts, coca production in Colombia continued to increase.

In 1999, concerned with the growing strength of the guerrillas and the continued flow of drugs northward to the United States, the Colombian and U.S. governments devised Plan Colombia. Proponents of the Plan in Washington and Bogotá claimed its successful implementation would end Colombia's civil war, revive the nation's economy, and drastically curtail cocaine production. In order to implement the $7.5 billion Plan, the government of Colombia requested $3.5 billion in international aid to supplement $4 billion of its own funding.

On January 11, 2000, President Clinton proposed a two-year $1.6 billion aid package as the initial U.S. contribution to Plan Colombia. With minimal debate, Congress approved $1.3 billion in July 2000, making Colombia the third-largest recipient of U.S. military aid in the world behind Israel and Egypt. With more than 70 percent of the U.S. aid earmarked for state security forces, Clinton was providing Colombia with the same level of military support the Salvadoran army received from the Reagan administration during the 1980s. Meanwhile, in sharp contrast to its direct involvement in the Northern Ireland and Middle East peace processes, the Clinton administration offered little support for Pastrana's peace initiative.

President Clinton flew to Cartagena, Colombia, on August 30, 2000, to symbolically deliver to Pastrana the $1.3 billion in U.S. aid. However, perhaps more symbolic than the aid delivery was the fact that more than 20 U.S. corporate executives arrived in Cartagena on the same day to meet with U.S. and Colombian government officials. Among the executives were Gary Drummond, CEO of Drummond Mining; Robert Hefner, CEO of the Seven Seas oil company; Mariella Nahao, vice-president of the energy firm Enron; Duane Ackerman, Bell South Corporation's CEO; and Liz Clairborne's CEO, Paul Charron.

The U.S. business leaders were in Cartagena to show their support for the economic component of Plan Colombia—essentially a continuation of the neoliberal economic policies imposed on Colombia by the IMF. The presence of the corporate executives in Cartegena illustrated that the $1.3 billion in U.S. taxpayer money is not so much an aid package for Colombia as a subsidy for Corporate America. Most of the money will wind up in the profit columns of numerous U.S. defense contractors that vigorously lobbied Congress for passage of the aid bill. These companies received contracts for the manufacture and servicing of military hardware to be used to safeguard the economic interests of other U.S. corporations doing business in Colombia.

Among the companies profiting are United Technologies, to the tune of $228 million for 18 Sikorsky Black Hawk helicopters, and Textron of Texas, in the amount of $60 million to upgrade Vietnam-era Huey helicopters.[40] The helicopters and other weaponry—as well as the training of three new Colombian army battalions by U.S. Special Forces—are being used against the guerrillas, not only to eradicate coca at its source, but in the hope of providing a more stable business environment for U.S. corporations. U.S. businesses operating in Colombia, especially oil and mining companies, stand to benefit if the military aid eventually leads to diminished rebel attacks on their Colombian interests. One company that has repeatedly been targeted by guerrillas is Occidental Petroleum, whose 490-mile Caño Limón-Coveñas oil pipeline was bombed 170 times in 2001.[41]

All of the companies benefiting from Plan Colombia are very well connected in Washington. United Technologies and Textron donated almost $2 million to Republican and Democratic campaigns between 1996 and 1998.[42] Democratic Senator Christopher Dodd of Connecticut was a staunch supporter of the aid package, which called for 18 Sikorsky Black Hawk helicopters to be built in his home state. Former Vice-President Al Gore owns some $500,000 in Occidental stock, while his father was the company's vice-president and a board member for decades. Furthermore, Occidental's chairman, Ray Irani, donated $100,000 to the Democratic National Committee in 1996 just two days after he slept in the Lincoln Bedroom of the White House.[43]

DynCorp, Military Professional Resources Inc. (MPRI), and other "mercenary" companies that hire U.S. veterans to conduct drug war operations in Colombia under State Department contracts also stand to benefit from this massive subsidization of Corporate America. DynCorp is a Virginia-based Fortune 500 company that was formed after World War II at the behest of President Harry Truman to provide jobs for ex-combatants and to make use of leftover war materiel. The company's current contract with the State Department calls for former U.S. military personnel working for DynCorp to pilot fumigation planes and helicopter gunships in Colombia, with the stipulation that Colombians operate the guns.

In December 2000, former U.S. ambassador to Colombia Myles Frechette addressed the issue of contracting MPRI to perform drug-war operations, admitting, "It's very handy to have an outfit not part of the U.S. Armed Forces. Obviously, if somebody gets killed or whatever, you can say it's not a member of the armed forces. Nobody wants to see American military men killed."[44] In fact, at least four DynCorp "civilian" personnel have been killed in the line of duty with minimal press coverage in the United States. In reality, Washington's use of ex-military personnel to conduct operations in Colombia's combat zones is little different than deploying U.S. troops—it is still U.S. taxpayer dollars funding direct U.S. military involvement in a foreign civil war. One of the most disturbing aspects of Washington's use of private contractors to perform combat-related duties is that it allows the president to wage war in Colombia without being held accountable by the U.S. Congress and the American people.

The implementation of Plan Colombia will ensure increased access for multinational corporations to Colombia's extensive natural and human resources, including oil, natural gas, coal, minerals, and a relatively industrialized workforce. The paramilitaries, who are allied with the U.S.-funded Colombian army, in turn are responsible for a majority of the massacres and forced displacement that makes mineral-rich Colombian real estate available for exploitation.

Plan Colombia and the Drug War

The initial objective of Plan Colombia is for the Colombian government to gain control of the entire country, some 40 percent of which is controlled by guerrilla forces. Proponents intend to achieve this goal by utilizing U.S.-trained Colombian army battalions, U.S.-supplied helicopter gunships and U.S.-piloted fumigation planes to target FARC-controlled, coca-growing regions of southern Colombia. According to the government, peasant farmers can avoid becoming targets of the aerial fumigation by choosing to participate in alternative crop programs, while aid will be made available to those *campesinos* forced to flee their homes and land as a result of the fumigation and violence.

Upon closer examination, Plan Colombia's true objective is the preservation of the political, social, and economic status quo in Colombia by means of a "carrot and stick" strategy. As is evident from the initial installment of overseas aid—the $1.3 billion U.S. aid package—the Plan intends to utilize a huge stick while offering a tiny carrot. The stick is the more than 70 percent of U.S. aid earmarked for state security forces and counternarcotics operations. The remainder constitutes the carrot: eight percent to alternative development projects; six percent to human rights programs; four percent to the displaced; two percent to judicial reform; and less than one percent to support the peace process.[45]

The European Union (EU) has been asked to provide additional funding, but many EU countries are apprehensive because of the Plan's emphasis on a military solution to what they see as political, social, and economic problems. It is this neglect of the hardships faced by the 68 percent of rural Colombians who live in poverty that concerns the Plan's critics.[46] In February 2001, the European Parliament voted 474-1 against supporting Plan Colombia, suggesting greater emphasis be placed on solving the underlying issues that have fueled the drug trade and the armed conflict. Many European critics believe Plan Colombia's reliance on a U.S.-sponsored war against the FARC will only deepen Colombia's social and economic crisis. They are also concerned that when the United States has completed the military phase of the Plan, Europe will be left to clean up the mess. The EU has distanced itself from Plan Colombia by not getting involved in the fumigation campaign and instead limiting its funding—some $300 million—to supporting President Pastrana's peace process and development projects.

Washington also faced strong opposition at the October 2000 Defense Ministers Summit held in Manaus, Brazil, which was attended by U.S. Secretary of Defense William Cohen and the defense ministers of several South American nations. Prior to the summit, Colombia's neighbors, especially Venezuela, Ecuador, and Panama, had denounced the militaristic nature of Plan Colombia, fearing it would destabilize the region by forcing guerrillas, drug production, and refugees to flee to neighboring countries. Venezuelan President Hugo Chávez had gone so far as to claim that it "could lead us to a Vietnamization of the whole Amazon region."[47]

At the summit, Deputy Undersecretary of Defense James Bodner strongly criticized Colombia's neighbors for their lack of support for U.S. involvement in Colombia and declared that Washington would go it alone if necessary. João Herrmann Neto of the Brazilian Chamber of Deputies dubbed this "typical American superiority."[48]

Many civic organizations inside Colombia have also voiced objections to the militaristic nature of the U.S. aid package. At the conclusion of an October 2000 peace conference held in San José, Costa Rica, representatives from more than 100 international and Colombian NGOs, along with leaders of the ELN, issued a statement condemning Plan Colombia's emphasis on a military solution. Jorge Rojas, leader of a coalition of Colombian NGOs known as Peace Colombia, called for a 100-day moratorium on aerial fumigation during which time alternative strategies could be developed.

Washington was seeking to implement an alternative strategy of its own when it called on the Colombian government to approve the use of a mycoherbicide called *Fusarium Oxysporum* in Plan Colombia's fumigation campaign. Critics claim that the use of this powerful fungus could not be restricted to coca plants and would not only wreak environmental havoc in Colombia's fragile ecosystem, but also constitute biological warfare. Plans to test the fungus against marijuana plants in Florida were abandoned "after environmentalists and a state official warned that it could mutate, spread rapidly, and kill off other plants including food crops."[49] The Colombian government has so far refused to succumb to U.S. pressure regarding the use of *Fusarium Oxysporum*.

Despite global opposition to Washington's escalating role in Colombia, the initial installment of U.S. aid was delivered after President Clinton waived the aid package's human rights conditions on August 22, 2000. During Congressional hearings on the aid bill, some members of Congress had insisted that the Colombian government be required to meet certain human rights conditions. However, these requirements were rendered irrelevant by a clause in the aid package that permitted the president to waive them if he deemed it to be in the interest of U.S. national security. According to the U.S. State Department, Colombia failed to meet six of the seven human rights conditions. Carlos Salinas, director of government relations for Amnesty International, said Clinton's waiver "speaks to the lack of political will on the part of the United States with regard to human rights."[50]

As a strategy for solving the drug trafficking problem, Plan Colombia will not drastically affect the availability of narcotics in the United States. History has shown that even if the military assault against the FARC and peasant coca growers in southern Colombia is successful, it will only be a temporary setback for the drug trade. For example, when coca cultivation was suppressed in Peru and Bolivia in the early 1990s, it simply moved to Colombia.

Much of the increased coca cultivation has occurred in FARC-controlled regions of southern Colombia, especially in the department of Putumayo. The dramatic increase in coca cultivation has enabled the FARC to become the largest and best-equipped guerrilla army in Latin American history. Consequently, Putumayo was selected as the first target of Plan Colombia's new U.S.-trained army battalions.

Critics of Plan Colombia were concerned about the Colombian army's relationship with paramilitary forces in Putumayo. The AUC announced its arrival in the region in 1998 with a series of massacres that left more than 100 people dead. Since its arrival, the paramilitaries have not only worked closely with the Colombian army's Putumayo-based 24th Brigade, it has even "paid monthly salaries to local army and police officials based on rank. Captains received between $2,000 and $3,000. Majors received $2,500 and lieutenants $1,500."[51] In April 2000, a local AUC leader known as Comandante Wilson admitted that the paramilitaries and the army routinely exchange coordinates of their fighters' whereabouts. He also claimed that the AUC and the army formulated Plan Colombia's long-term strategy together because "Plan Colombia would be almost impossible without the help of the [paramilitary] self-defense forces."[52] Even though the paramilitaries, as their leader Carlos Castaño has admitted, are largely funded through the drug trade, they have been willing to sacrifice some of this income in support of Plan Colombia as long as the FARC remain the principal target of the drug war.

Ignoring the many critics of Plan Colombia, Washington and Bogotá launched the initial fumigation campaign on December 19, 2000. Two of the Colombian army's U.S.-trained anti-narcotics battalions spent six weeks in Putumayo protecting fumigation planes from ground attacks. By early February, with 62,000 acres of coca destroyed, the politicians and generals in Washington and Bogotá were calling Plan Colombia's initial campaign a success. But on the ground in Putumayo it was clear that more than just coca had been eradicated. Many *campesinos* watched in horror as the deadly mist drifted down and stuck to everything in sight. They saw their food crops turn brown, wilt, and slowly die. And they watched their children and animals become sick.

Inevitably, serious questions were raised about the fumigation campaign. An estimated 85,000 gallons of the herbicide glyphosate were dumped onto Putumayo's coca fields by planes that routinely sprayed at altitudes as high as 100 feet. The Monsanto Company— the manufacturer of Round-Up Ultra, the form of glyphosate used in Colombia—cautions against aerial application at altitudes greater than ten feet above the targeted crops. According to Monsanto, higher altitudes increase the risk of drift, which should be avoided because "even very small amounts of Round-Up herbicide brands may damage crops if allowed to drift into fields adjoining the target area."[53]

Questions have also been raised regarding the destructiveness of glyphosate, which has been used to fumigate illicit crops in Colombia since 1996. Ricardo Vargas, a researcher for Acción Andina, an organization studying drug policy in the Andes, claims that glyphosate has proven extremely effective because the dosage being used is five liters per acre, a concentration level that far exceeds the recommended one liter per acre.[54]

Another reason the herbicide is so destructive is because it is being mixed with an adjuvant called Cosmo-Flux 411F. According to Colombian agronomist Doctor Elsa Nivia, "Cosmo-Flux substantially increases the biological activity of the agro-chemicals, allowing better results with smaller doses."[55] But the fumigation campaign in southern Colombia is not using Cosmo-Flux with smaller doses of glyphosate; it is adding it to a dosage that is five times greater than recommended.

In January 2001, in the midst of Plan Colombia's initial fumigation campaign, the U.S. State Department insisted that glyphosate was "the only chemical currently used for aerial eradication."[56] But U.S. officials were later forced to admit that the glyphosate was in fact being mixed with Cosmo-Flux 411F. Apparently, unable to wage biological warfare with *Fusarium Oxysporum*, Washington instead found a way to turn a common herbicide into a chemical weapon.

Some of the families who fled the fumigation are struggling to survive in the small town of San Miguel, situated on the Colombian side of the border with Ecuador, while others have sought refuge inside Ecuador. According to Cecilia Ramírez, who with her husband and three children abandoned the family's farm in La Dorada after it had been fumigated, "Everything was killed—maize, yucca, plantains, everything."[57] Comandante Enrique, chief of Putumayo's paramilitary forces and a supporter of Plan Colombia, admitted, "If you go to San Miguel you can find *campesinos* who don't have food and money because the fumigation was indiscriminate and killed licit and illicit crops."[58]

Doctors at the local hospital in La Hormiga, a town of 35,000 in the heart of the Guamuez Valley, witnessed some of the human health consequences of the fumigation campaign. According to Doctor Edgar Perea, "I have treated people with skin rashes, stomach aches and diarrhea caused by the fumigation. And I have treated five children affected by the fumigation in the past 25 days. I don't know how many the other doctors have treated."[59] In June 2001, Imperial Chemical Industries (ICI), a British company that produced a key ingredient in Cosmo-Flux, announced it would no longer participate in the fumigation campaign because of reports about Colombian children becoming ill from the chemicals.

Prior to the launching of the Plan Colombia offensive in Putumayo, the Colombian government offered *campesinos* technical assistance, $1,000 in cash, and a promise that their farms would not be fumigated if they agreed to switch from coca to alternative crops. Some *campesinos* accepted the offer while others, distrustful of a government that had repeatedly failed to deliver on past promises, steadfastly refused. As one La Hormiga resident explained, "Historically, the government has never helped anyone here. People helped themselves and with coca the economy became good. Now the government wants to help, but people are afraid it will ruin the economy."[60]

Local concerns proved to be justified when, six months after the initial fumigation, most farmers still had not received any of the promised financial aid or technical support regarding the cultivation of alternative crops. The poor administration of the alternative crop program was illustrated by the dismal failure of one project that imported thousands of chickens from the Andean highlands. The chickens, unaccustomed to Putumayo's hot and humid tropical climate, died soon after their arrival.

Adding injury to insult, many of the small farmers who had already uprooted their coca bushes stood by helplessly as the aerial fumigation killed their newly planted legal crops. But according to Colonel Blas Ortiz of the army's 24th Brigade, the fumigation campaign only targeted "industrial sized" coca farms of 25 acres or more. The colonel also claimed, "One of the techniques used by the big coca growers is to grow two acres of yucca or plantains in the middle of 125 acres of coca. These two acres don't belong to the *campesinos*, they belong to the big coca grower. They use this strategy to avoid being fumigated."[61]

Doctor Ruben Darío Pinzón of the National Plan for Alternative Development (PLANTE), the government agency in charge of the alternative crop program, expressed sympathy for the *campesinos*. "Growers financed by PLANTE have been fumigated because they are in a small area in the middle of coca growers. It is impossible to protect them because the pilots can't control exactly where they fumigate. They fumigate the whole area." The indiscriminate nature of the fumigation campaign has led many to call for a greater emphasis on manual eradication, which would avoid damaging food crops. Doctor Pinzón claims, "PLANTE is fighting to end fumigation in the six municipalities in which we are working so we can start the process of alternative crops and then begin negotiations with other towns."[62]

Most coca farming occurs in remote areas that lack the roads and infrastructure required for transporting perishable legal crops to distant cities and ports. When asked if PLANTE intends to help *campesinos* get their alternative crops to distant markets, Doctor Pinzón lamented, "At this time it is not possible to propose such an economic plan. It is desirable that the government subsidize some items like they do in the United States and Europe, but in Colombia it's not possible because we do not have the money."[63]

If the number of *campesinos* turning to alternative crops continues to increase, production will likely surpass local demand and drive prices down, and impoverished *campesinos* will once again face the same economic problems that forced them to turn to coca cultivation in the first place.

In recent years, Colombia has also become the largest supplier of heroin to the United States. Many of the poppies, which provide the raw ingredient for the production of heroin, are grown in remote regions of the Andean highlands. Some of Colombia's indigenous communities supplement the meager subsistence provided by their traditional crops of maize, yucca, coffee, beans, potatoes, wheat, and onions with poppy cultivation. The reason, according to a young Yanacona leader, William Armando Palechor, is that there is no commerce available for the traditional food crops, which are difficult to transport to markets. As a result, says Palechor,

"Indigenous communities have adopted illicit crops as traditional crops."[64]

Some of the 16,000 Guambiano Indians living in the Andean highlands around the town of Silvia in the department of Cauca cultivate poppies on small plots of land behind their mud-brick houses. They also grow high-altitude food crops in fields spread across the steep mountainsides. While poppies constitute only a small percentage of the land under cultivation, they provide a far more reliable income for poor indigenous families. The Guambianos sell the valuable opium latex to traffickers from Cali, who willingly journey to the mountains to purchase the raw material they need to process heroin. In contrast, many legal food crops are only used for subsistence because of their low market value and the difficulty of transporting them from remote mountain communities to towns and cities.

Like many of the region's indigenous groups, the Guambianos have experienced repeated incursions onto their reservation by armed groups seeking to expand their control over the drug trade. According to the vice-governor of the Guambiano communities, Fabio Calambas, "We have problems with the armed groups who invade and conduct activities in our territories without authority. They occupy our territories with violence and then when the public forces arrive we are caught in the middle of the fighting."[65]

Because illicit crops have escalated the conflict on the reservation, community leaders understand the need to discourage their cultivation. In an attempt to deter individual Guambiano families from cultivating poppies and encourage a return to a more communal system of agriculture, the local Guambiano council has tried to develop crop substitution agreements with the government. But one such project in which the Guambianos bred fish in ponds was devastated by the aerial fumigation of illicit crops. Calambas claims,

"We have suffered fumigations that contaminated the water and destroyed the trout crop. The few that survived were never bought. These fumigations have affected our crops and our lifestyle."[66]

It is evident that, unless provided with viable economic alternatives, highland indigenous communities will continue to grow poppies, and *campesinos* in the tropical lowlands will continue to cultivate coca. This was clearly illustrated in November 2001, when the fumigation planes, attack helicopters, and ground troops returned to Putumayo eight months after the initial spraying when satellite surveillance revealed that thousands of peasant farmers had replanted their coca crops.

There is also evidence that Plan Colombia's fumigation campaign is driving coca and poppy cultivation back to Peru where, not only is illicit crop production thriving once again in the Upper Huallaga Valley, but there is also a resurgence in guerrilla warfare being waged by the Shining Path rebel group.[67] Finally, the futility of Washington's drug war tactics is driven home by the fact that, despite the destruction of thousands of acres of coca and poppies over the past decade, the availability and price of cocaine and heroin in U.S. cities have remained constant.

The Peace Process

In June 1998, the Conservative candidate Andrés Pastrana won the Colombian presidential election, campaigning on a platform of peace. His message resonated with millions of Colombians tired of the escalating violence. Newspaper photographs during the campaign of Pastrana meeting with Manuel "Sureshot" Marulanda, the legendary 70-year-old leader of the FARC and a veteran of the peasant self-defense groups formed during *La Violencia*, led many to believe he was capable of negotiating a peace agreement with the guerrillas.

In November 1998, President Pastrana withdrew 2,000 soldiers and police from a 16,200 square mile area in southern Colombia known as the *zona de despeje* (cleared zone) in preparation for peace talks with the FARC. However, the talks would be conducted without a cease-fire agreement, meaning hostilities between government forces and the rebels would continue outside the zone.

Over the years to come, the absence of a cease-fire would prove to be the Achilles heel of the fledgling peace process. Any of Colombia's armed actors—including those not participating in the talks—had the power to derail negotiations by launching attacks. The FARC, for instance, recalled its peace negotiators after paramilitaries disrupted the opening of the talks on January 7, 1999, by launching a four-day offensive that resulted in the deaths of 136 civilians. The FARC declared that talks would not continue until the government made a serious attempt to combat the death squads, as well as government and military officials linked to them.

Over the next two years, the FARC repeatedly withdrew from negotiations because of the government's failure to dismantle the paramilitaries. On the other side of the table, the government grew frustrated, as did many Colombians, with the rebels' unwillingness to offer any serious peace concessions.

Two months after the initial breakdown, President Pastrana forced into retirement two senior army generals suspected of having paramilitary ties. This brought the FARC back to the negotiating table, and on May 6, 1999, both sides agreed to a 12-point agenda for the peace talks. Among the issues to be discussed were agrarian reform, economic and social restructuring, the exploitation of the country's natural resources, the human rights situation, military reform, and international relations.

The state of the country's economy, particularly the unemployment crisis, was the first topic addressed. From January 31 to February 16, 2000, the government's peace commissioner and a delegation of FARC guerrillas toured Sweden, Norway, Switzerland, Italy, France, and Spain, where they observed and discussed the social and economic structures of western European democracies. Following the European tour, a series of public conferences were held in the rebel safe-haven, which allowed Colombian citizens, civic organizations, unions, and business groups to discuss the economy with the guerrillas.

What little progress was being made in the peace process came to a halt on November 15, 2000, when the FARC again broke off talks because of the government's failure to effectively combat the paramilitaries. The Colombian army, whose generals had never been happy with the decision to cede territory to the guerrillas, began a troop buildup on the perimeter of the safe-haven hoping to receive the green light to retake the zone if President Pastrana decided not to issue a renewal by the January 30, 2001 deadline.

The residents of the zone's principal town, San Vicente del Caguán, had become accustomed to the sight of AK-47-toting rebels patrolling the streets, shopping in their stores, and eating in local restaurants. Many of the townsfolk enjoyed living in the rebel safe-haven, not necessarily because they supported the FARC, but because the removal of the other armed groups had dramatically decreased the level of violence. The feeling in San Vicente was that "most Colombians would love to live like this."[68]

Locals were worried that terminating the zone would once again subject them to the violence that still plagued the rest of the country. The mayor of San Vicente, Néstor Ramírez, was concerned that a failure to renew the zone would bring an end to the peace process and the arrival of paramilitaries.[69] Lelo Celis, a local taxi driver, echoed the mayor's fears: "Pastrana has to renew the zone, otherwise Carlos Castaño and his paramilitaries will follow the army into San Vicente and target all those believed to have collaborated with the FARC during the past two years."[70] His words proved tragically prescient. In October 2001, Celis was killed by paramilitaries.

Pastrana traveled to the rebel safe-haven for an eleventh-hour meeting with FARC leader Manuel Marulanda. After intense negotiations, both sides reached an agreement to resume peace talks with discussions focusing on a prisoner exchange and a possible cease-fire. This agreement was followed on February 7 by a request from Pastrana to newly-elected President George W. Bush that the United States join in the talks. However, the U.S. president refused the request, citing the FARC's refusal to hand over those responsible for the 1999 killing of three U.S. human rights activists who were working with the U'wa tribe in northern Colombia.

Washington also claimed that the FARC was using the zone to increase its drug profits by forcing *campesinos* to grow more coca. FARC Comandante Simón Trinidad denied that the rebel group was pressuring peasants into cultivating coca crops:

> The campesinos grow illicit crops out of necessity. It is specifically a socio-economic situation. They are obligated to cultivate illicit crops because of a government that has neglected them for many years. We have made it clear that we will not take the food out of the mouth of the poor campesino. The economic model of the Colombian state has caused this problem, and it is the state that has to fix it. We are the state's enemy, not their anti-narcotics police.[71]

Finally, on June 28, 2001, the peace process achieved its first tangible result: a prisoner exchange. FARC negotiators agreed to hand over 363 captured soldiers and police in return for the release of 11 sick rebels being held in government prisons. But the country's renewed optimism about the peace process was short-lived. On August 13, the government arrested three members of the Irish Republican Army (IRA) after they left the rebel safe-haven and charged them with training FARC guerrillas in urban terrorism.

Despite this setback, Pastrana renewed the zone for another four months after the FARC agreed to end its practice of conducting mass kidnappings on Colombia's highways—a tactic dubbed "miracle fishing," for the small chance of actually catching someone worthy of a ransom. In return, the government agreed to crack down on paramilitary activity and emphasized that any future renewal of the rebel safe-haven would depend on the FARC agreeing to a cease-fire.

Meanwhile, the 5,000-strong ELN was seeking its own safe-haven in which to conduct peace talks with the government. The ELN made its initial request for a demilitarized zone during secret talks with the Colombian government in Caracas, Venezuela, in February 1999. The talks were short-lived as the rebels broke off negotiations when the government refused their zone request. It wasn't until April 25, 2000, that Bogotá and the ELN finally agreed to create an "encounter zone" in the northeastern department of Bolívar that would host peace talks and a National Convention.

According to Antonio García, military commander of the ELN, all sectors of Colombian society would participate in the National Convention, including industrialists, political organizations, trade unions and church groups. "There is a lot of interest in the National Convention because it comes from the idea that the solution to the conflict must be a collective one, that we must unite our efforts to create a national consensus in favor of change." In reference to how the National Convention would address the ongoing process of globalization, García stated, "Any project that changes society must include the idea that we need an economic model that serves the people and society, not the other way around."[72]

In February 2001, thousands of local *campesinos* blockaded the country's major north–south highways to protest the imminent creation of the ELN's safe-haven in southern Bolívar. President Pastrana publicly accused the AUC of organizing and financing the protests, which effectively cut the country in half. Thousands of peasant protesters at the blockades enjoyed a conspicuous abundance of food supplies, with large trucks arriving daily to refill their water containers.

Three days into the protest President Pastrana ordered the army to clear the blockades and reopen the highways. The commander of Barrancabermeja's Nueva Granada Battalion (and School of the Americas graduate), Lieutenant Colonel Hernán Moreno, warned, "It is the National Police who deal with public order problems, not the army. The moment we go in to save the police we will have to shoot the protesters, and it's not constitutional to shoot the people."[73] The impending use of excessive force by the army was averted when the demonstrators peacefully terminated the blockade after the government agreed to discuss the implementation of the demilitarized zone with local community leaders.

On May 30, despite the fact the government had yet to reach an agreement that satisfied all parties involved, Pastrana ordered the withdrawal of troops from a 1,120 square mile area in southern Bolívar in preparation for peace talks. On April 9, the ELN accused the government of doing nothing to halt a paramilitary offensive launched against the ELN in the area cleared of government troops. It soon became apparent that the military strength of the AUC was seriously threatening the ELN's control over the region. When

Pastrana did send the army back into the demilitarized area, it was to fight the guerrillas, not the paramilitaries.

In August 2001, President Pastrana, under pressure from local officials in southern Bolívar, proposed that peace talks with the ELN be moved from the yet-to-be created encounter zone to a location outside the country. The ELN immediately rebuffed Pastrana's suggestion, claiming the president was reneging on their previous agreement. To the surprise of many Colombians, Pastrana abruptly terminated talks with the ELN and took the offensive by publicly assailing the rebel group and their "obstinate position."[74] The guerrillas responded by declaring they had no further interest in participating in negotiations until after Pastrana's term was to end in August 2002. However, following further military setbacks at the hands of the Colombian army and the paramilitaries, ELN leaders soon changed their minds and agreed to peace talks without any preconditions. In November 2001, rebel and government negotiators began formal peace talks in Havana, Cuba—along with representatives from France, Norway, Spain, Switzerland and Cuba—aimed at reaching a cease-fire agreement.

While there was renewed hope regarding Bogotá's negotiations with the ELN, the government's talks with the FARC hit yet another stumbling block. Following the terrorist attacks against the United States on September 11, 2001, the rhetoric emanating from Washington shifted from emphasizing the FARC's role in the drug trade to the rebel group's place on the U.S. State Department's list of terrorist organizations. At an October 10 House subcommittee hearing on terrorism, the State Department's Coordinator for Counterterrorism, Francis X. Taylor, labeled the FARC "the most dangerous international terrorist group based in this hemisphere."[75] The U.S. ambassador to Colombia, Anne Patterson, echoed Taylor's comments, "My government is concerned by the use of the

[FARC] demilitarized zone as a base for terrorist acts."[76]

In response to the FARC's suspected IRA links and Washington's anti-terrorism rhetoric, the Colombian army beefed up its forces around the perimeter of the rebel safe-haven and the government banned foreigners from entering the zone without authorization from Bogotá. The FARC again walked away from the negotiating table, threatening not to return until the government withdrew the army and allowed free access in and out of the zone. The guerrillas, fearful of being attacked by the United States as part of its war on terrorism, also demanded that Pastrana publicly declare that the FARC is not a terrorist organization.

Meanwhile, public opinion polls showed the Colombian people were losing patience with the oft-stalled peace talks, while President Pastrana's record-low approval ratings signified a lack of confidence in the nation's leader.

In the weeks leading up to the January 20, 2002, deadline for renewal of the rebel safe-haven, Pastrana finally got tough with the FARC. The Colombian president demanded that the rebels return to the negotiating table and agree to a timetable for cease-fire talks or he would send in the army to retake the zone. Hours before the midnight deadline, government and rebel negotiators announced that they had set a timetable to reach a cease-fire agreement by April 7. However, there was a significant chasm between the two sides regarding what territory the FARC would retain control over during a cease-fire. The rebels wanted their 60 fronts to remain in control of their strongholds throughout the country, essentially creating dozens of small rebel safe-havens. For its part, the government was demanding that all rebels move to the FARC's zone in southern Colombia where the peace talks were being held. It was a military concession the FARC was unwilling to make as long as right-wing paramilitaries remained free to move into vacated rebel-controlled regions. The geurrillas again called on the government to dismantle the paramilitaries, while also demanding that Bogotá establish a system of unemployment compensation for the country's jobless and order all U.S. military advisors to leave Colombia. The government in turn called on the FARC to cease all kidnapping and extortion.

Not only did Bogotá and Washington ignore the FARC's call for the removal of U.S. military advisors, but in February, the Bush administration actually sought an escalation of the U.S. role in Colombia by proposing a $98 million counterterrorism aid package. According to Curt Struble of the State Department's Bureau of Western Hemisphere Affairs, "The $98 million in foreign military financing is not for counternarcotics. . . . Instead, this money is to assist units of the Colombian armed forces that are responsible for protecting a critical piece of infrastructure, the Caño Limón pipeline."[77] If approved by Congress, this new aid would expand U.S. involvement beyond counternarcotics to counterterrorism and even counterinsurgency as the Bush White House seeks to utilize taxpayer dollars to protect the risky foreign investments of U.S. corporations such as Occidental Petroleum.

On February 20, the peace process abruptly ended when President Pastrana ordered the Colombian military to invade the rebel zone in response to the FARC's hijacking of an airliner and the abduction of one of its passengers, Colombian Senator Jorge Gechen Turbay. Claiming the FARC's increased military activities showed they were not serious about achieving peace, Pastrana gave the guerrillas less than three hours notice of the impending military invasion, clearly violating a previous agreement that the government would give the rebels 48 hours to vacate the zone upon its termination.

In the first two days following Pastrana's suspension of the peace process, the Colombian air force, using U.S.-supplied A-37 jets and AC-47 bombers, flew at least 400 sorties against more than 80 targets in the rebel safe-haven. The ensuing days saw thousands of ground troops, supported by U.S.-supplied Black Hawk helicopters, retake the principal towns in the former rebel zone. The FARC responded by bombing infrastructure throughout the country, while residents of the former safe haven feared that the return of the army would also bring paramilitary death squads intent on "cleansing" the region of suspected rebel sympathizers.

In reality, there was little chance of the peace process succeeding because both the Colombian government and the FARC were unwilling or unable to compromise. The imposition of economic austerity programs on Colombia by the IMF as part of Washington's post-Cold War globalization process did not allow Bogotá to give realistic consideration to the sort of economic and social restructuring called for by the FARC. While the FARC's increased military strength meant rebel negotiators did not have to settle for any agreement that failed to achieve their stated revolutionary goals of far-reaching political, social and economic reforms.

For its part, the Bush administration responded to the end of the peace process by requesting the removal of restrictions that limit U.S. aid to counternarcotics operations. The Bush White House also asked Congress for a $35 million emergency supplement to provide immediate aid to the Colombian military in advance of the administration's $98 million anti-terrorism aid request for 2003. Some of the supplemental aid would go to Colombian army units whose mission is to protect the Caño Limón-Coveñas oil pipeline. Clearly concerned with instability in the Middle East and Venezuela—the primary sources of oil for the United States—Bush is using the broader justification of the war on terrorism to protect U.S. energy interests by expanding the U.S. role in Colombia to include increased support for the Colombian army's counterinsurgency war against the FARC.

While there is little doubt regarding the global reach of terrorist organizations such as al-Qaeda, there is no evidence that the FARC is anything but one of the armed actors in Colombia's long and tragic domestic conflict. Significantly, while Washington focuses on combating the FARC, it chooses mostly to ignore the AUC, which is also on the State Department's list of Foreign Terrorist Organizations.

Conclusion

Over the past fifty years, the FARC has evolved from a small band of armed peasants during *La Violencia* into a powerful military force of 17,000 fighters that controls approximately 40 percent of Colombia. A U.S. Defense Intelligence Agency (DIA) report issued in November 1997 concluded, "The Colombian Armed Forces could be defeated within five years unless the country's government regains political legitimacy and its armed forces are drastically restructured."[1] The U.S. aid package has managed to greatly strengthen Colombia's armed forces. However, in the eyes of many Colombians, little has been done to legitimize the government in Bogotá.

In 1999, former U.S. drug czar General Barry McCaffrey echoed the findings of the DIA report when he claimed that Colombian democracy was being seriously threatened by the growing military strength of the guerrillas.[2] One can only assume that McCaffrey's concept of "democracy" included social order "maintained" under a military state of siege, impunity for paramilitary forces that regularly massacre the civilian population, the routine assassination of political candidates in opposition to the ruling elite, a judicial system paralyzed by fear, and thousands of peasants and indigenous peoples whose only economic means of survival is illicit coca and poppy cultivation.

The principal candidates for the May 2002 presidential elections offer little hope to those Colombians seeking far-reaching political, social, and economic reforms. The election promises to be politics as usual because none of the leading candidates pose any serious threat to the entrenched Colombian oligarchy. President Pastrana's failed peace process and record-low approval ratings negatively affected the election chances of fellow Conservative Juan Camillo Restrepo who, while polling less than one percent, dropped out of the race in mid-March after his party's dismal showing in congressional elections.

The current political climate has resulted in a rare opening for independent presidential candidates. One such candidate is frontrunner Alvaro Uribe Vélez, an extreme rightist whose father was killed by the FARC. Uribe's past ties to "self-defense" groups during his tenure as governor of Antioquia, his hard-line rhetoric towards the rebels, and his call for foreign troops to help combat the guerrillas, render him an unlikely peacemaker.

The Liberal Party candidate, Horacio Serpa, has infused his campaign with populist rhetoric about implementing social and economic reforms. But in reality, he is closely tied to the country's traditional political and economic elite. Also, his call for a government crackdown on right-wing paramilitaries rings hollow in light of recent revelations that he secretly and illegally met with Carlos Castaño in Cali in 1996.

For the first time in Colombian electoral history, there are two women presidential candidates. However, not only are Noemí Sanín and Ingrid Betancourt longshots in the presidential race, both of them are products of Colombia's traditional political class. Betancourt's campaign, which focused on the country's rampant political corruption, was in limbo following her February 23 kidnapping by the FARC. The rebels have said they would release Betancourt and five Colombian senators in return for the release of 200 imprisoned guerrillas, but the government has ruled out any possibility of swapping kidnapped politicians for rebel prisoners.

Luis Eduardo Garzón is the lone candidate who possesses the political will and vision to implement systemic changes in Colombia. But given Colombia's history of assassinating reformist candidates, the former leader of the country's largest union will be lucky to make it to election day alive. The government's last-minute discovery of an AUC plot to kill Garzón on the day he officially launched his campaign illustrates why many on the left have abandoned the electoral process and joined the ranks of the guerrillas. Colombia's Interior Minister, Armando Estrada, lamented this fact following the attempt on Garzón's life, "We have already paid dearly for having closed the doors on the left. The extermination of the members of the UP (Patriotic Union) is something we Colombians are paying a high price for."[3]

Estrada's concerns are illustrated by the FARC's refusal to allow members of its new clandestine political organization, the Bolivarian Movement, to run for office until the government has dismantled the paramilitaries. Even if the threat to leftist candidates is eliminated and someone willing to seriously address Colombia's social and economic inequalities is elected president, his or her hands would still be tied by the neoliberal policies imposed on the country by the U.S.-dominated IMF. Furthermore, with the implementation of the Free Trade Area of the Americas (FTAA) slated for 2005, the influence of multinational corporations in Colombia's political and economic affairs will continue to increase.

To a large degree, Colombia's future lies in the hands of Washington's policymakers. President George W. Bush's $625 million Andean Regional Initiative, despite a slight increase in social and development funding, promises to continue the militaristic drug war policies of the Clinton administration. Providing counterterrorism and counterinsurgency aid to the Colombian military, primarily to combat the FARC while mostly ignoring the AUC, will only further fuel Colombia's violence. There is also the risk that such a continuing escalation of U.S. military involvement will eventually lead to a direct intervention of U.S. troops in Colombia's civil conflict.

An alternative course of action would have Washington using its leverage with the Colombian military to force the dismantling of the paramilitary groups and end the aerial fumigation of illicit crops. Bogotá could then demand that the guerrillas stop all kidnapping and agree to a cease-fire. This would provide a favorable environment in which the government and the rebels, along with the business community, trade unions, and civic groups could seriously address the country's political, social, and economic issues. One such issue is agrarian reform, which must include the return of prime agricultural lands currently owned by drug traffickers to thousands of displaced peasant farmers.

At the same time, by redirecting military aid to help develop Colombia's rural infrastructure and implementing effective alternative crop programs, the United States could provide critical assistance to reforming the chronic inequities that fuel the civil war and the drug trade. Here at home, shifting the emphasis from law enforcement to much-needed drug education and treatment programs would go a long way toward reducing the demand for illegal drugs.

In order for such a peace process to succeed, it would also be essential that Washington dispense with the IMF-imposed austerity measures that severely restrict the ability of Colombians to develop a social and economic model acceptable to all sectors of society. Finally, with the dismantling of the paramilitary death squads, the resultant political opening would allow candidates of all political persuasions to safely and effectively campaign for office.

Regrettably, as of this writing, it appears unlikely that Washington will maneuver along these lines, even if doing so promised to bring an end to Colombia's drug production and the decades of violence. Such a comprehensive strategy for peace would inevitably interfere with U.S. corporate interests in Colombia and diminish Washington's political and economic hegemony in the region. Colombia's ruling elite and the military and paramilitary forces that protect and further its interests would also, in all likelihood, be reluctant to negotiate away its birthright of a stranglehold on the nation's wealth.

As for the FARC and ELN, they would be obliged to fully cooperate with a peace proposal that addresses the issues for which they claim to be fighting or risk losing what little legitimacy they have left. Ultimately, the real beneficiaries of such reform-minded policies would be the millions of Colombians caught in the middle of the conflict who want nothing more than a just peace.

Recommended Reading

Bergquist, Charles, Ricardo Penaranda, and Gonzalo Sanchez, eds. *Violence in Colombia: The Contemporary Crisis in Historical Perspective.* Wilmington, Del.: Scholarly Resources, 1992.

———. *Violence in Colombia 1990-2000: Waging War and Negotiating Peace.* Wilmington, Del.: Scholarly Resources, 2001.

Braun, Herbert. *Our Guerrillas, Our Sidewalks: A Journey into the Violence of Colombia.* Niwot: University Press of Colorado, 1994.

Bushnell, David. *The Making of Modern Colombia: A Nation in Spite of Itself.* Berkeley: University of California Press, 1993.

Carrigan, Ana. *The Palace of Justice: A Colombian Tragedy.* New York: Four Walls Eight Windows, 1993.

Clawson, Patrick L., and Rensselaer W. Lee III. *The Andean Cocaine Industry.* New York: St. Martin's, 1998.

Drexler, Robert W. *Colombia and the United States: Narcotics Traffic and a Failed Foreign Policy.* Jefferson, N.C.: McFarland & Company, 1997.

Giraldo, Javier S.J. *Colombia: The Genocidal Democracy*. Monroe, Me.: Common Courage, 1996.

Human Rights Watch. *Generation Under Fire: Children and Violence in Colombia*. New York: Human Rights Watch, 1994.

——. *Colombia's Killer Networks: The Military-Paramilitary Partnership and the United States*. New York: Human Rights Watch, 1996.

——. *War Without Quarter: Colombia and International Humanitarian Law*. New York: Human Rights Watch, 1998.

——. *The Sixth Division: Military-Paramilitary and U.S. Policy in Colombia*. New York: Human Rights Watch, 2001.

Kline, Harvey F. *State Building and Conflict Resolution in Colombia 1986-1994*. University of Alabama Press, 1999.

Randall, Stephen J. *Colombia and the United States: Hegemony and Interdependence*. Athens: University of Georgia Press, 1992

Ruiz, Bert. *The Colombian Civil War*. Jefferson, N.C.: McFarland & Co., 2001.

Safford, Frank, and Marco Palacios. *Colombia: Fragmented Land, Divided Society*. Oxford: Oxford University Press, 2001.

Sánchez, Gonzalo, and Donny Meertens. *Bandits, Peasants, and Politics: The Case of "La Violencia" in Colombia*. Austin: University of Texas Press, 2001.

Scott, Peter Dale, and Jonathan Marshall. *Cocaine Politics: Drugs, Armies, and the CIA in Central America*. Berkeley: University of California Press, 1998.

Notes

Fifty Years of Violence

1. In reality, the law not only failed to alleviate the inequitable distribution of land, it actually sanctioned the property claims of many large landowners. See, Catherine LeGrand, "Agrarian Antecedents of the Violence" in Charles Bergquist, Ricardo Penaranda and Gonzalo Sanchez, eds. *Violence in Colombia: The Contemporary Crisis in Historical Perspective* (Wilmington, Del.: Scholarly Resources, 1992), p. 42.

2. Robert W. Drexler, *Colombia and the United States: Narcotics Traffic and a Failed Foreign Policy* (Jefferson, N.C.: McFarland & Company, 1997), p. 62.

3. Ernesto "Che" Guevara, *The Motorcycle Diaries: A Journey Around South America* (London: Verso, 1995), p. 144.

4. For a fascinating account of the siege of the Palace of Justice, see Ana Carrigan, *The Palace of Justice: A Colombian Tragedy* (New York: Four Walls Eight Windows, 1993).

5. Benjamin Keen, *A History of Latin America* (Boston: Houghton Mifflin, 1996), p. 514.

6. Human Rights Watch/Americas, *Colombia's Killer Networks: The Military-Paramilitary Partnership and the United States* (New York: Human Rights Watch, 1996), p. 17.

7. Javier Giraldo S.J., *Colombia: The Genocidal Democracy* (Monroe: Common Courage, 1996), p. 85.

8. Ricardo Vargas Meza, "The FARC, the War and the Crisis of State," *NACLA Report on the Americas*, Mar./Apr. 1998, p. 24.

9. Commission for the Study of Violence, "Organized Violence" in Bergquist, et al., eds. *Violence in Colombia*, p. 268.

10. Mark Chernick, "The Paramilitarization of the War in Colombia," *NACLA Report on the Americas*, Mar./Apr. 1998, p. 30.

11. Human Rights Watch/Americas, *Colombia's Killer Networks*, p. 25.

12. Ibid, p. 23-24.

13. Giraldo S.J., *Colombia*, p. 49.

14. Chernick, "The Paramilitarization of the War in Colombia," p. 32.

15. Mauricio Aranguren Molina, *Mi Confesión: Carlos Castaño Revela Sus Secretos* (Bogotá: Editorial La Oveja Negra, 2001), p. 205.

16. Frank Smyth and Maud S. Beelman, "Pentagon Trained Troops Led by Officer Accused in Massacre," Center for Public Integrity, Mar. 20, 2000, online.

17. Military Forces of Colombia, "Order No. 200-05/91: Organization and Operation of Intelligence Networks," cited in Human Rights Watch/Americas *Colombia's Killer Networks*, p. 109.

18. Human Rights Watch/Americas, *Colombia's Killer Networks*, p. 33.

19. Ibid, p. 35.

20. Douglas Farah, "U.S. Force Training Troops in Colombia," *Washington Post*, May 25, 1998, p. A1. It is difficult to understand how U.S. Special Forces were the primary beneficiaries of counterinsurgency training conducted with poorly trained, poorly equipped, and poorly motivated Colombian soldiers, but so went the U.S. logic.

21. Human Rights Watch/Americas, *Colombia's Killer Networks*, p. 93.

22. "SOA Graduates: Notorious Graduates—Colombia," School of the Americas Watch, online. See also, "SOA Graduates in the News 2000/2001: Colombia," School of the Americas Watch, Spring 2001, online.

Colombia and the New World Order

1. Patrick L. Clawson and Rensselear W. Lee III, *The Andean Cocaine Industry* (New York: St. Martin's Press, 1998), 52.

2. International Information Programs, "Fact Sheet: Colombia, U.N. Discussing Anti-Coca Mycoherbicide Cooperation," *U.S. Department of State*, Jul. 17, 2000, online.

3. George H.W. Bush, "Statement on Trade Initiatives for the Andean Region," George Bush Presidential Library and Museum, Nov. 1, 1989, online.

4. "Colombia at a Glance—1999," The World Bank Group, May 29, 2000, online.

5. Mike Fox, "Bush Argues for Budget Deficit," *BBC News*, Jan. 8, 2002, online. In January 2002, U.S. president George W. Bush declared that the United States "might have to run deficits in times of war, in times of a national emergency or in times of recession, and we're still in all three."

6. James Wilson, "Colombia Abandons ETB Sale," *Financial Times*, Sept. 22, 2000, online.

7. Karl Royce, "Isagen Posts US $2.03 mn Profits," *Business News Americas*, Apr. 3, 2001, online. See also, "ISA Registers US $60.7 mn Jan-Sep Profits," *Business News Americas*, Nov. 7, 2001, online.

8. Joseph E. Stiglitz, "The Failure of the Fund: Rethinking the IMF Response," *Harvard International Review*, Summer 2001, p. 16.

9. James Attwood, "Auditor Requests Govt. to Unplug Power Privatizations," *Business News Americas*, Mar. 7, 2001, online.

10. Mark Schapiro, "Big Tobacco: Uncovering the Industry's Multibillion-Dollar Global Smuggling Network," *The Nation*, May 6, 2002, p. 13.

11. Ibid, p. 13.

12. Ibid, p. 15.

13. Barbara Clements, "Starbucks Announces Its Earnings Set Record," *The News Tribune*, Nov. 16, 2001, online.

14. "Minister: IMF, Multilateral Banks Have Impoverished Latin America," *Hoover's Online*, Mar. 5, 2002, online.

15. "Human Rights Watch World Report 2001," Human Rights Watch, 2001, online.

16. Ibid.

17. Ibid.

18. Global IDP Project, "The Issue of Land Plays an Intimate Role With the Phenomenon of Displacement (1994–1999)," 2000, Norwegian Refugee Council, online.

19. "Colombia Refugee Tide Grew in 2001—Study," Reuters, Feb. 12, 2002, online.

20. Luis Hernández, interview with author, Feb. 18, 2001, Barrancabermeja, Santander, Colombia.

21. Claudia Marcela Barona, interview with author, Feb. 21, 2001, Bogotá, Colombia.

22. María Eugenia Martínez, interview with author, Jun. 20, 2000, Bogotá, Colombia.

23. Observatorio de los Derechos Humanos en Colombia, "El Secuestro en Cifras," Presidencia de la Republica de Colombia, 2001, online.

24. Central General Staff of the FARC-EP, "Law 002 Concerning Taxation," FARC-EP, Mar. 2000, online.

25. Diana Roa, interview with author, Mar. 7, 2002, Bogotá, Colombia.

26. Jorge Eliécer Rodríguez and Aniana Sierra Rodríguez, interview with author, Mar. 8, 2002, Vereda Aquisí, Antioquia, Colombia. In fact, the Colombian army routinely performs demining in order to protect its soldiers in the field but refuses to do so for mine-plagued communities, as is required as part of its 1997 Mine Ban Treaty obligations.

27. Agence France Presse, "More Than 300 Indians Killed This Year in Colombia: Activist," *Colombia Labor Monitor*, Nov. 25, 2001, online.

28. Lawrence P. Meriage, "House Government Reform Subcommittee on Criminal Justice, Drug Policy and Human Resources: Hearing on Colombia," U.S. House of Representatives, Feb. 15, 2000, online.

29. Ebaristo Tegria Uncaria, interview with author, Jun. 19, 2000, Bogotá, Colombia. Royal Dutch Shell, citing human rights and public relations concerns, has since backed out of the project.

30. Meriage, "House Government Reform Subcommittee," Feb. 15, 2000, online.

31. Régulo Madero Fernández, interview with author, Feb. 19, 2001, Barrancabermeja, Santander, Colombia.

32. Mateo, interview with author, Feb. 18, 2001, Barrancabermeja, Santander, Colombia.

33. Madero Fernández, Feb. 19, 2001.

34. Javier, interview with author, Feb. 18, 2001, Barrancabermeja, Santander, Colombia.

35. "Protect Community Leaders in Barrancabermeja," Colombia Support Network, Feb. 19, 2000, online.

36. Bureau of Democracy, Human Rights and Labor, "Country Reports on Human Rights Practices 2001: Colombia," U.S. Department of State, Mar. 4, 2002, online. See also, "Colombia: Annual Survey of Violations of Trade Union Rights (2001)," International Confederation of Free Trade

Unions, online.

37. David Bacon, "The Colombian Connection: U.S. Aid Fuels a Dirty War Against Unions," *In These Times*, Jul. 23, 2001, p. 13.

38. Dudley Althaus, "These People Are Disposable," *Houston Chronicle*, Oct. 20, 1997, online.

39. "Sixty Journalists Killed in 2001," World Association of Newspapers, Jan. 22, 2002, online. See also, "Americas 2000: Colombia," Committee to Protect Journalists, 2001, online.

40. Adam Isacson, "The 2000-2001 Colombia Aid Package By the Numbers," Center for International Policy, Jul. 5, 2000, online.

41. "Colombia Limón Oilpipe Down After Year's First Bomb," *Forbes*, Jan. 11, 2002, online.

42. Andrew Reding, "The View From Latin America—The Closer You Are to Colombia, the Worse the New Aid Plan Looks," World Policy Institute, Aug. 16, 2000, online.

43. Damian Whitworth, "Gore Campaign Stumbles Over Threat to Tribe," *Times of London*, Mar. 13, 2000, online.

44. Paul de la Garza and David Adams, "Special Report: The War in Colombia," *St. Petersburg Times*, December 3, 2000, p. 1A.

45. Colombia Project, "The Contents of the Colombia Aid Package," Center for International Policy, Jan. 26, 2001, online.

46. *This is Not Our War: Children and Forced Displacement in Colombia* (Santafé de Bogotá: CODHES/UNICEF, 2000), p. 26.

47. "Venezuela's Chávez Warns Colombia Could Become Another Vietnam," CNN, Aug. 30, 2000, online.

48. "Latin Defense Ministers and U.S. Spar Over Plan Colombia," CNN, Oct. 18, 2000, online.

49. Sharon Stevenson and Jeremy Bigwood, "Drug Control or Biowarfare?" *Mother Jones*, May 3, 2000, online.

50. Elise Labott, Andrea Koppel, and Kelly Wallace, "Clinton OKs Colombia Aid Package Despite Country's Human Rights Abuses," CNN, Aug. 23, 2000, online.

51. Human Rights Watch, *The 'Sixth Division': Military-Paramilitary Ties and U.S. Policy in Colombia* (New York: Human Rights Watch, 2001), p. 22.

52. Ken Penhaul, "Drug War's Secret Alliance: Right-Wing Gunmen Say U.S.-backed Government Troops Helping Them Drive Rebels From Colombian Coca Fields," *San Francisco Chronicle*, Apr. 12, 2001, online.

53. Farm Source, "Product Usage: Round-Up Ultra," Monsanto Company, online.

54. Ricardo Vargas, *Fumigación y conflicto: Políticas antidrogas y deslegitimación del estado en Colombia* (Santefé de Bogotá: TNI/Acción Andina/Tercer Mundo Editores, 1999), p. 4.

55. Elsa Nivia, "Cosmo-Flux 411 F: Coadyuvante adicionado al Roundup Ultra en la erradicación forzosa de cultivos ilícitos en Colombia," Transnational Institute, Jan. 12, 2001, online.

56. Fact Sheet Released by the Bureau of Western Hemisphere Affairs, "United States Support for Colombia," Department of State, Jan. 17, 2001, online.

57. Cecilia Ramírez, interview with author, Feb. 8, 2001, San Miguel, Putumayo, Colombia.

58. Comandante Enrique, interview with author, Feb. 7, 2001, La Hormiga, Putumayo, Colombia.

59. Doctor Edgar Perea, interview with author, Feb. 10, 2001, La Hormiga, Putumayo, Colombia.

60. Gustavo, interview with author, Feb. 10, 2001, La Hormiga, Putumayo, Colombia.

61. Colonel Blas Ortiz Rebolledo, interview with author, Feb. 5, 2001, Santana, Putumayo, Colombia.

62. Doctor Ruben Dario Pinzón, interview with author, Feb. 6, 2001, Puerto Asis, Putumayo, Colombia.

63. Ibid.

64. William Armando Palechor, interview with author, Mar. 5, 2002, Popayan, Cauca, Colombia.

65. Fabio Calambas, interview with author, Mar. 6, 2002, Silvia, Cauca, Colombia.

66. Ibid.

67. Monte Hayes, "Thriving Peru Coca Hampers Drug War," Associated Press, Mar. 13, 2002, online.

68. Anonymous, interview with author, Jan. 28, 2001, San Vicente del Caguán, Caquetá, Colombia.

69. Néstor Leon Ramírez Valero, interview with author, Jan. 30, 2001, San Vicente del Caguán, Caquetá, Colombia.

70. Lelo Celis, interview with author, Jan. 29, 2001, San Vicente del Caguán, Caquetá, Colombia.

71. Comandante Simón Trinidad, interview with author, Jun. 14, 2000, Los Pozos, Caquetá, Colombia.

72. Liam Craig-Best, "An Interview With ELN Commander Antonio García," *Colombia Report*, Aug. 27, 2000, online.

73. Lieutenant Colonel Hernán Moreno, interview with author, Feb. 19, 2001, Barrancabermeja, Santander, Colombia.

74. "Pastrana Cuts Off Talks With ELN Rebels," CNN, Aug. 7, 2001, online.

75. Statement of Ambassador Francis X. Taylor, Coordinator for Counterterrorism, U.S. Department of State, "Committee on International Relations, Subcommittee on the Western Hemisphere, U.S. House of Representatives," U.S. House of Representatives, Oct. 10, 2001, online.

76. Discurso por la embajadora de los Estados Unidos en Colombia, Anne Patterson, "Nuevas relaciones de los Estados Unidos y Colombia," Center for International Policy, Oct. 25, 2001, online.

77. Curt Struble, "Briefing on FY 2003 International Affairs Budget," U.S. Department of State, Feb. 4, 2002, online.

Conclusion

1. Weekly News Update of the Americas, "Multilateral Invasion Force for Colombia?" *NACLA Report on the Americas*, May/Jun. 1998, pp. 46-47.

2. "U.S. Drugs Czar Says Colombian Democracy Under Threat," BBC News, Mar. 1, 1999, online.

3. James Wilson, "Colombia Uncovers Assassination Plans," *Financial Times*, Dec. 12, 2001, online.

Index